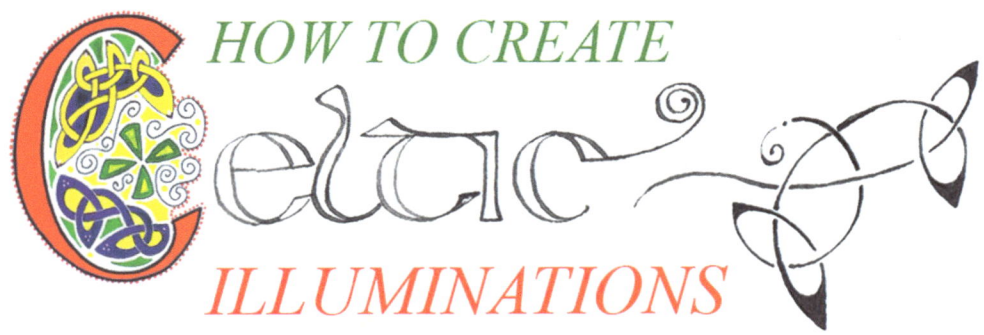

Revised Edition --- 2022

Jane Sullivan

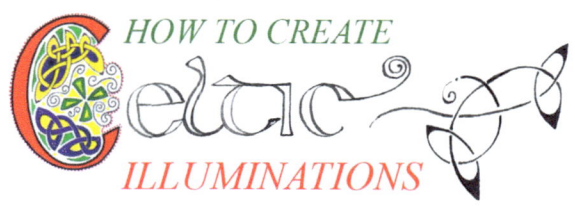

©2021   *Jane Sullivan*
www.calligrafee.com

Revised and corrected 2022

All rights reserved (including all forms of reproduction
or adaptation of text and images, in all forms, in all countries)

ISBN: 9798710297391

CONTENTS

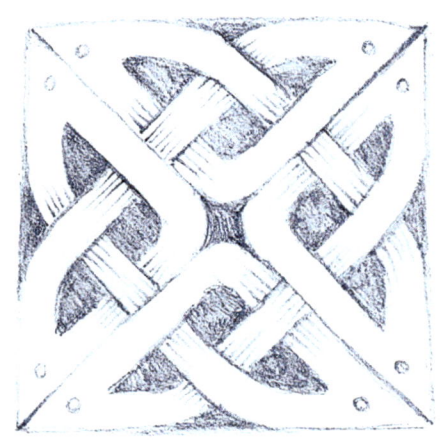
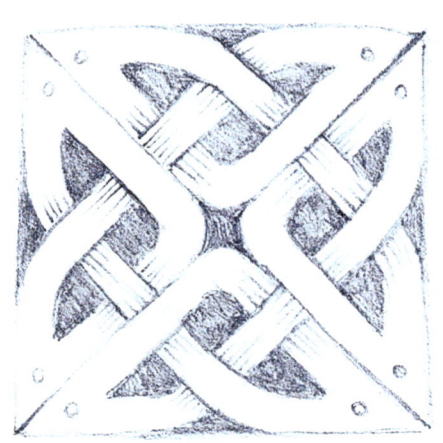

Chapter 1:
An Illuminated Alphabet
page 5

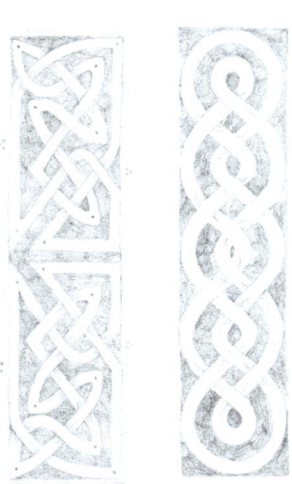
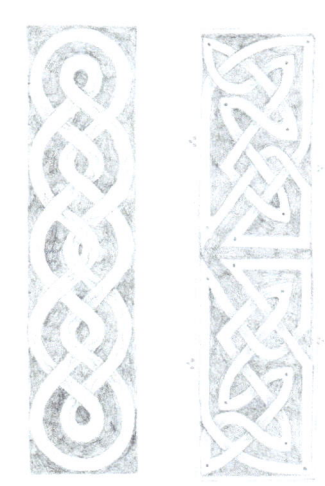

Chapter 2:
Interlace Using Cords and Animals
page 23

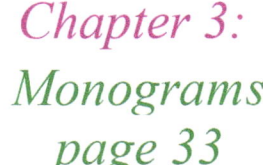

Chapter 3:
Monograms
page 33

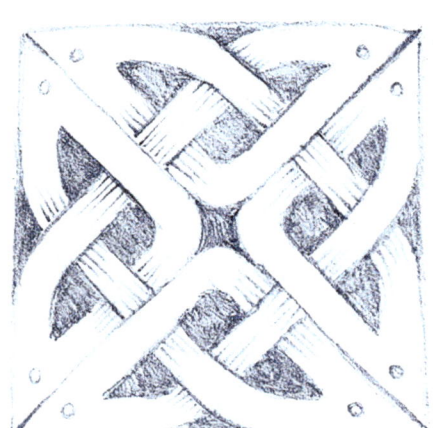
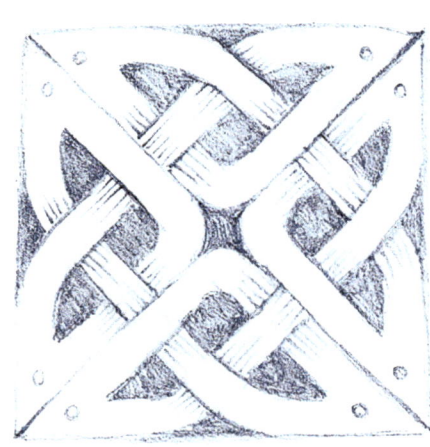

Chapter 4:
Carpet Page Projects
page 39

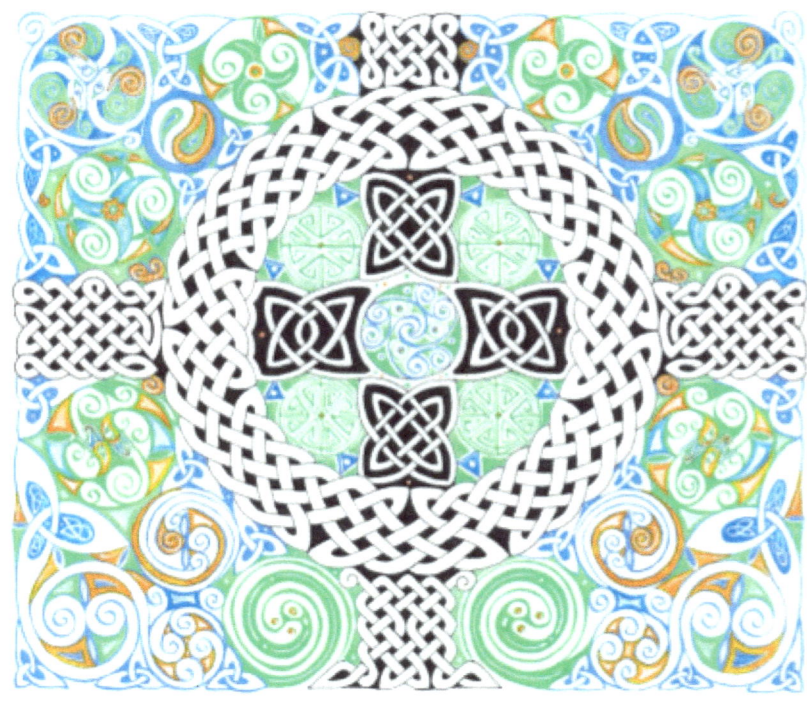

A note before we begin: The instructions on the following pages are rather concise and, unless you are already a practiced artist, they may seem to go a bit too quickly. If you find that you need more detailed explanations of some of these motifs, techniques or ideas, I suggest that you follow the clases of my On-Line Art School, which you will find on my web-site *calligrafee.com/en*: module 5 is all about Celtic Illuminations. The six video classes presented in that module will give you the chance to watch the creation of similar designs, and to follow along at your own pace.

However, if you study the images presented on the following pages, and take your time to copy and enjoy them, I'm sure you will be able to master these delightful, through sometimes complex, forms!

An Illuminated Alphabet

Insular Majuscule

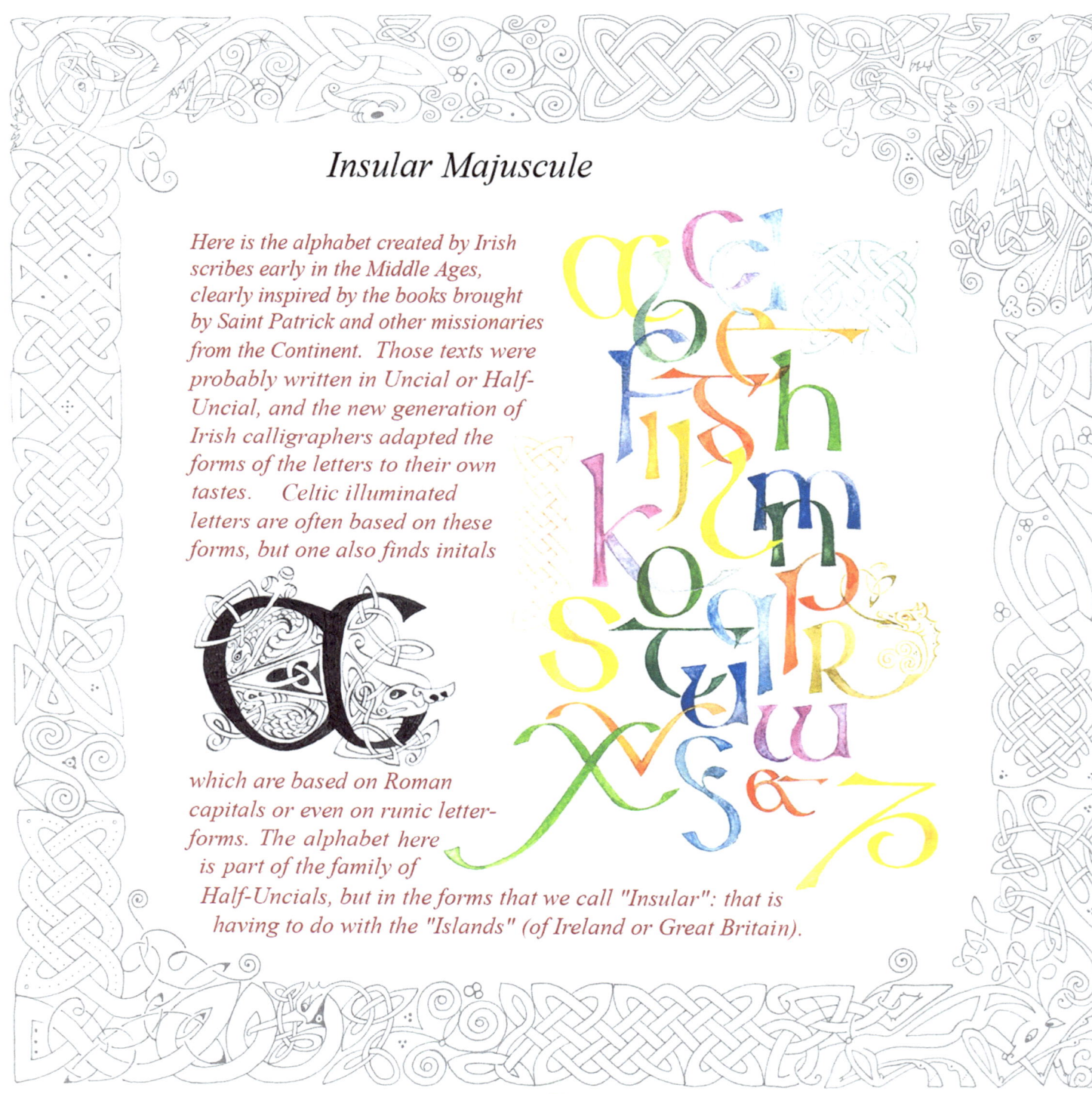

Here is the alphabet created by Irish scribes early in the Middle Ages, clearly inspired by the books brought by Saint Patrick and other missionaries from the Continent. Those texts were probably written in Uncial or Half-Uncial, and the new generation of Irish calligraphers adapted the forms of the letters to their own tastes. Celtic illuminated letters are often based on these forms, but one also finds initals which are based on Roman capitals or even on runic letter-forms. The alphabet here is part of the family of Half-Uncials, but in the forms that we call "Insular": that is having to do with the "Islands" (of Ireland or Great Britain).

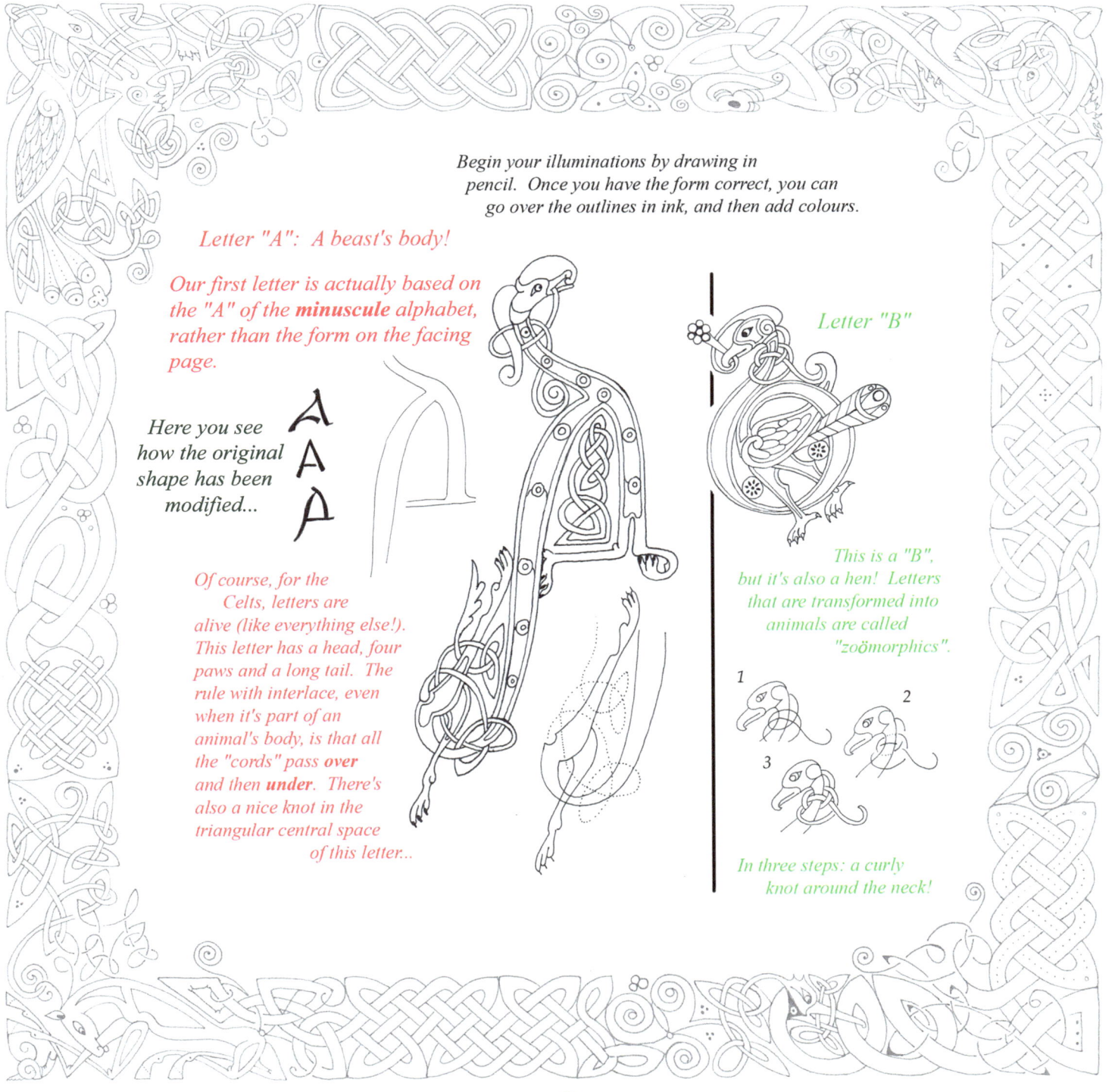

Begin your illuminations by drawing in pencil. Once you have the form correct, you can go over the outlines in ink, and then add colours.

Letter "A": A beast's body!

*Our first letter is actually based on the "A" of the **minuscule** alphabet, rather than the form on the facing page.*

Here you see how the original shape has been modified...

*Of course, for the Celts, letters are alive (like everything else!). This letter has a head, four paws and a long tail. The rule with interlace, even when it's part of an animal's body, is that all the "cords" pass **over** and then **under**. There's also a nice knot in the triangular central space of this letter...*

Letter "B"

This is a "B", but it's also a hen! Letters that are transformed into animals are called "zoömorphics".

In three steps: a curly knot around the neck!

With these three letters, you'll learn a little about colouring your
illuminations, more on knotwork, and also a new style of animal head.

Letter "C"

Here's a simple letter, but note that its form has very slight variations in thickness: especially at top and bottom, it becomes quite a bit thinner.

On the following page, you'll find suggestions, in three steps, on how to colour this initial.

Letter "D": hugs and kisses!

Like most of the letters presented in this book, **my** inspiration comes from the Book of Kells. In that marvelous manuscript, this is actually an illumination of **two** letters: D and I. For our alphabet, we will simply say that it's a "D" with a friend in its arms! At upper-right, you have the basic form of the letter, and at right the guide for its tail....

And here, at far left, is the rearing little *beast* in the centre of the "D"... and here is the form of the twirling knots around the lower left of the letter.

Letter "E"

This letter shows you an animal-head seen from above: a sort of dog-snake! But if you find this "E" rather **too** odd, take a look at the other forms for this letter on the following page...

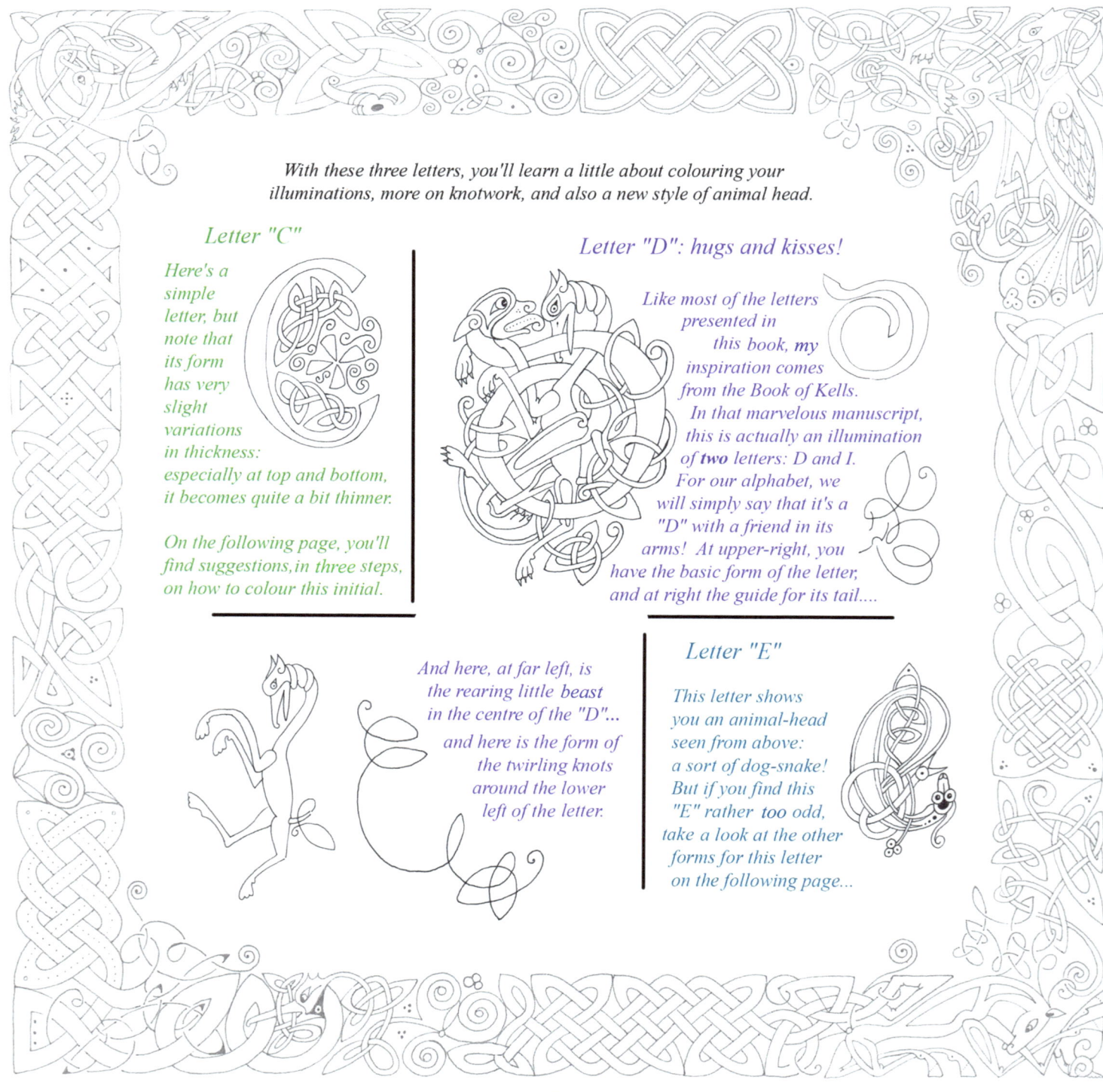

8

The Letter "C" in Colour: three steps in bright gouache paints

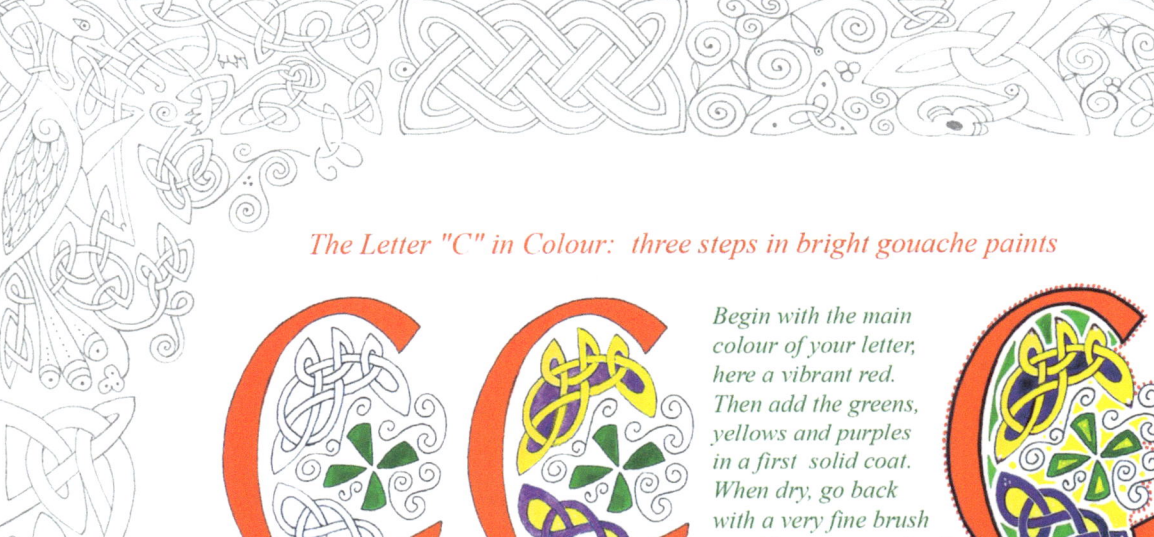

Begin with the main colour of your letter, here a vibrant red. Then add the greens, yellows and purples in a first solid coat. When dry, go back with a very fine brush to add one or two details such as dots or triangles over the first colours.

Finish with the painted shapes around the motifs and a series of tiny red dots all around the letter.

Three alternative forms of "E"

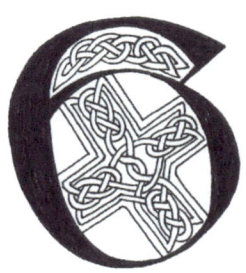

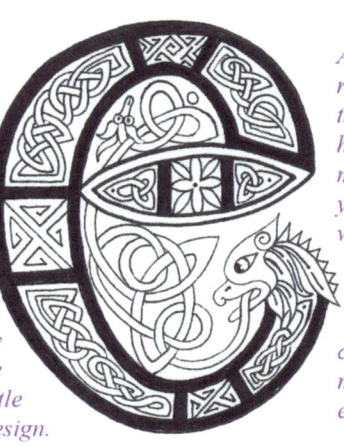

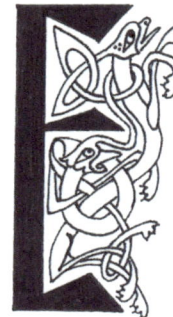

Variations for this letter abound. Above is a nicely rounded one with a large interior space for a little interlace cross design.

At left, another round "E", but this time with hollow compartments, inviting you to fill each with a different motif. And a lion-head to finish the bottom curve, its tongue making some extra knotwork!

Above is a more angular "E", with rather complicated inhabitants!

Letters "F", "G" and "H"

Letter "F"

The "F" at left is actually a fabulous animal-body, complete with forelegs (making the horizontal bar) and two hind-legs entangled with some looping knotwork! Draw the basic "F" form first, then transform the various parts into head and legs as desired. Erase the intersections of the knots to re-draw them with their overs-and-unders.

Letter "G"

The Celtic "G" is a strange shape at best, and here he is given a head as well, with a twisty tongue and another nice crescent-shaped wedge of interlace in the bow of the letter.

Letter "H"

The majuscule, initial "H" of our alphabet is more like a small "h" to our eyes. But here it becomes very majestic nonetheless, filled with busy knotwork of bird-forms. Details and close-ups of these forms are given on the next page...

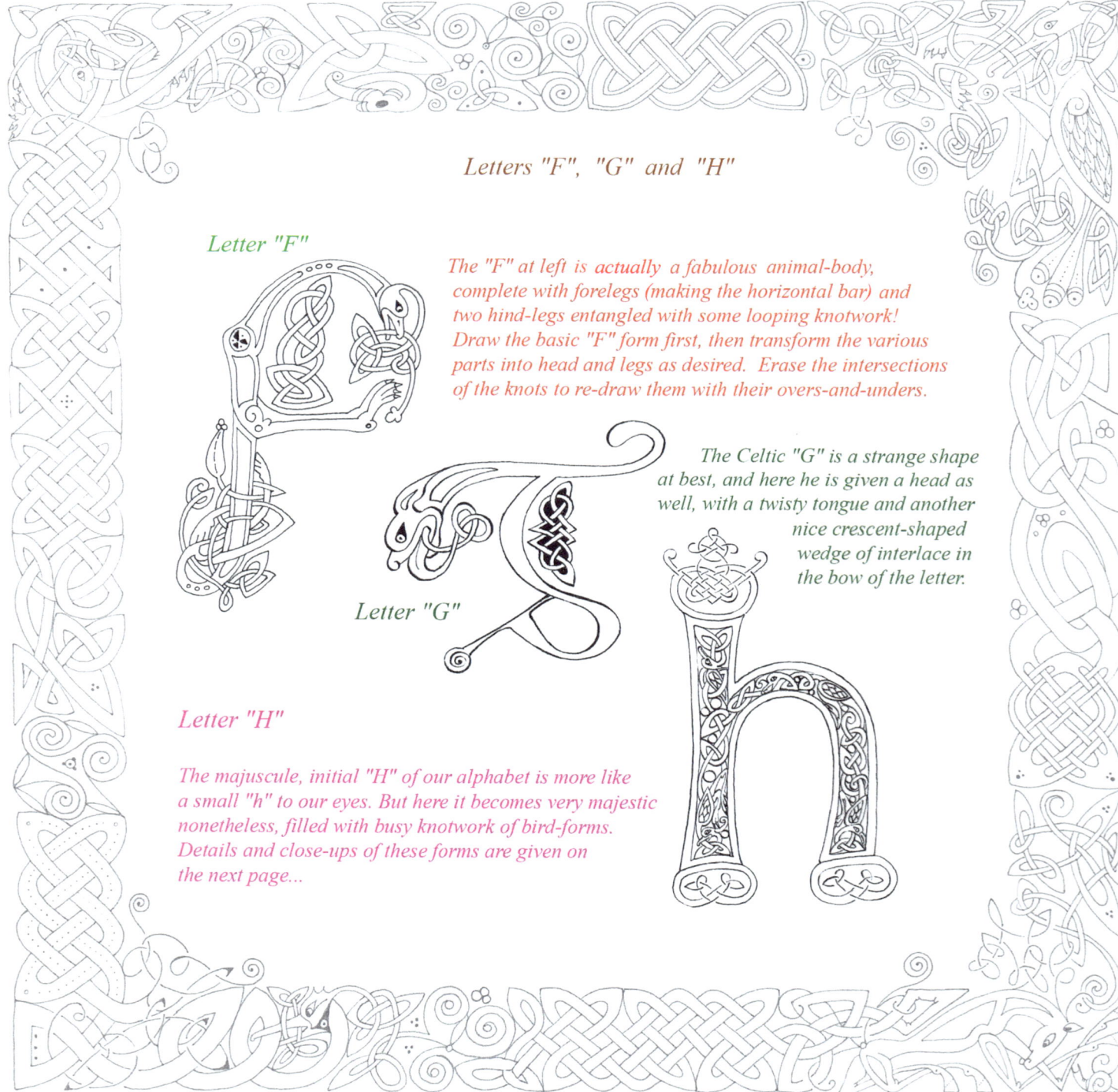

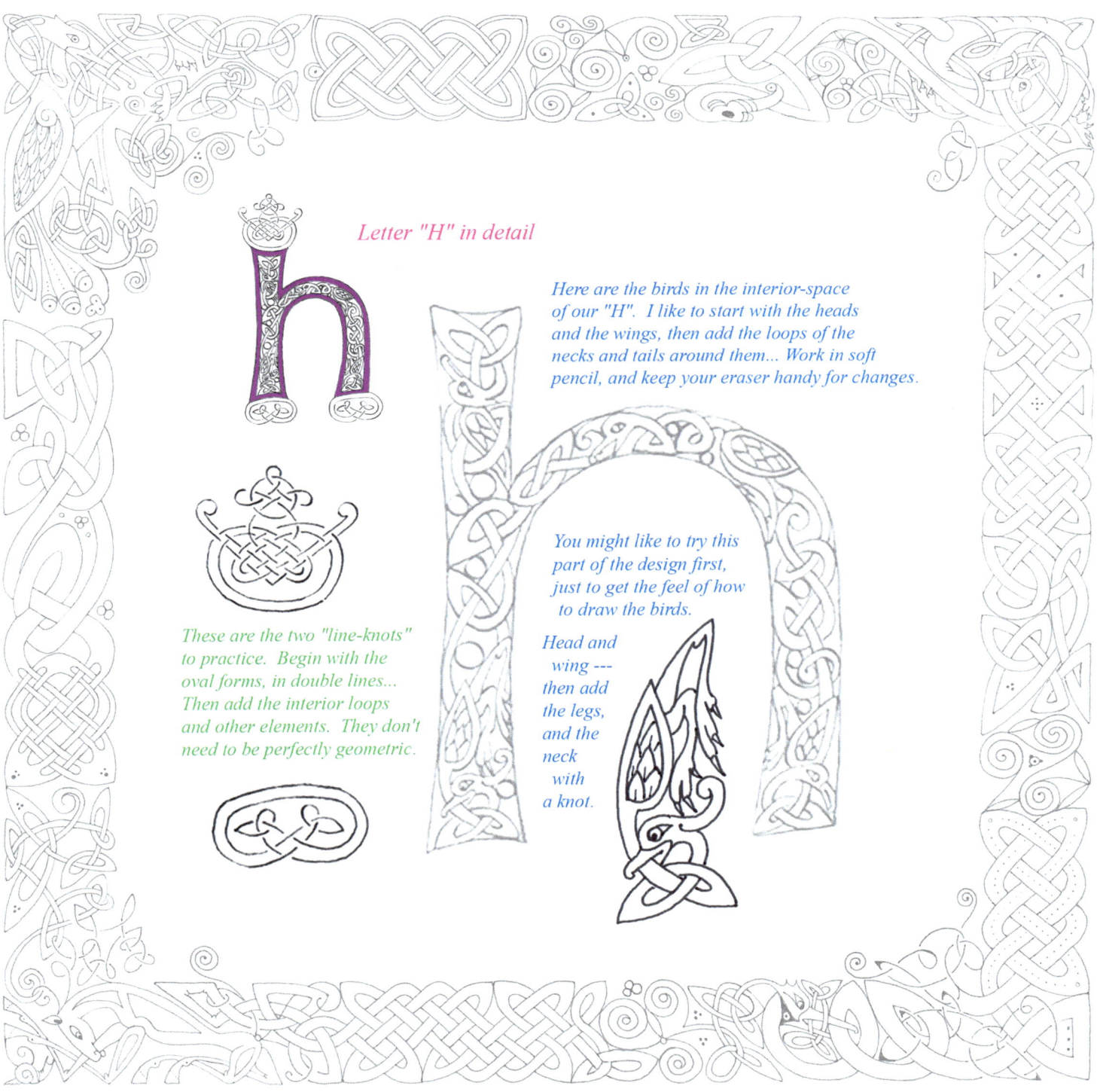

Letter "I"

Well, yes, this is a cat! But it's also the letter "I"... and a complicated letter at that (as the Celtic scribes so enjoy!) One could even extend the cat's nose a little more, to recall the "wedge" shape so characteristic of this alphabet.

Letter "J"

In the Middle Ages, the "I" and the "J" were one and the same letter; but here you have a slightly modified form to make the distinction between the two. The woven knotwork between the animal heads is just for fun! Below you have the steps.

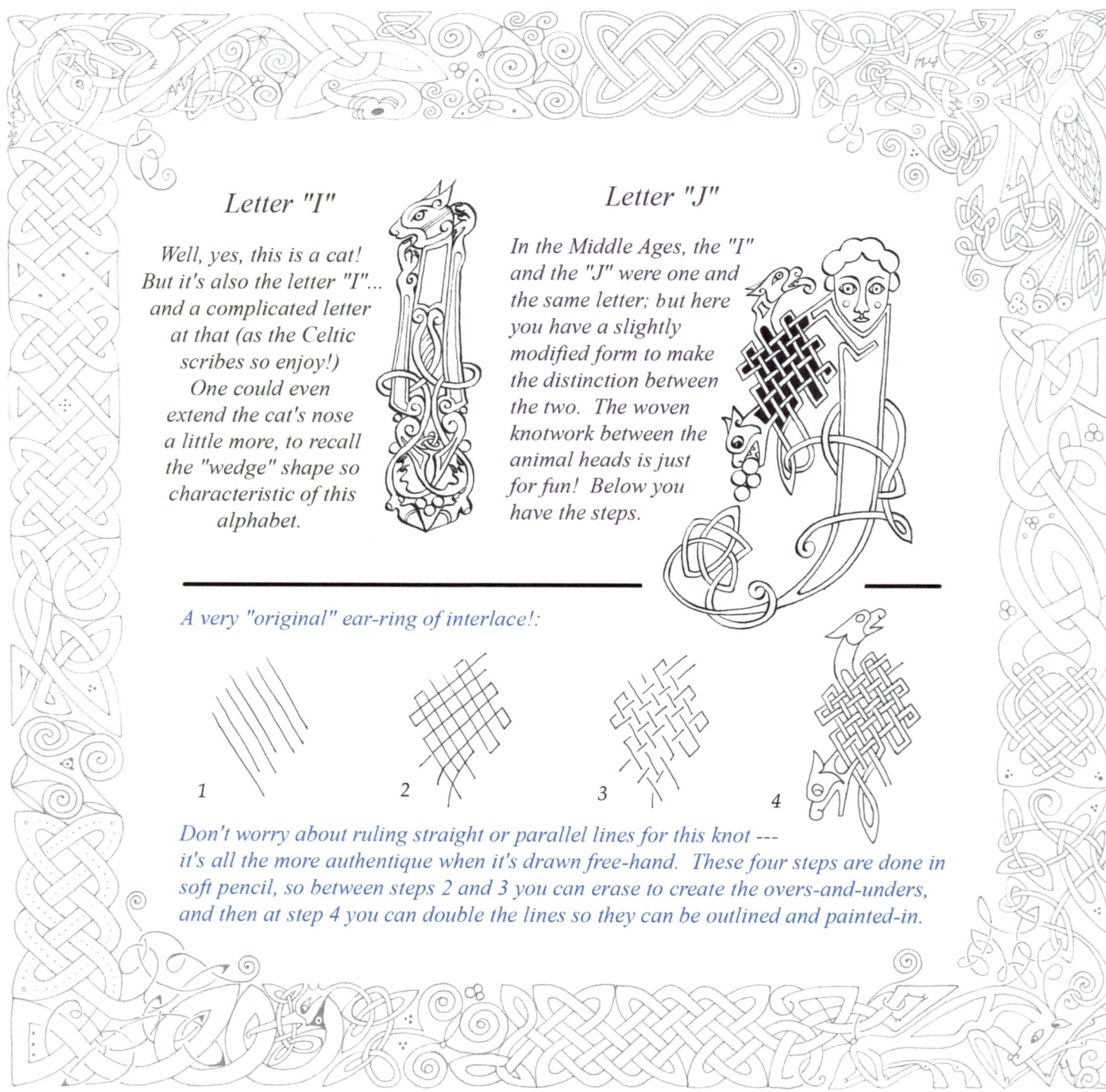

A very "original" ear-ring of interlace!:

1 2 3 4

Don't worry about ruling straight or parallel lines for this knot --- it's all the more authentique when it's drawn free-hand. These four steps are done in soft pencil, so between steps 2 and 3 you can erase to create the overs-and-unders, and then at step 4 you can double the lines so they can be outlined and painted-in.

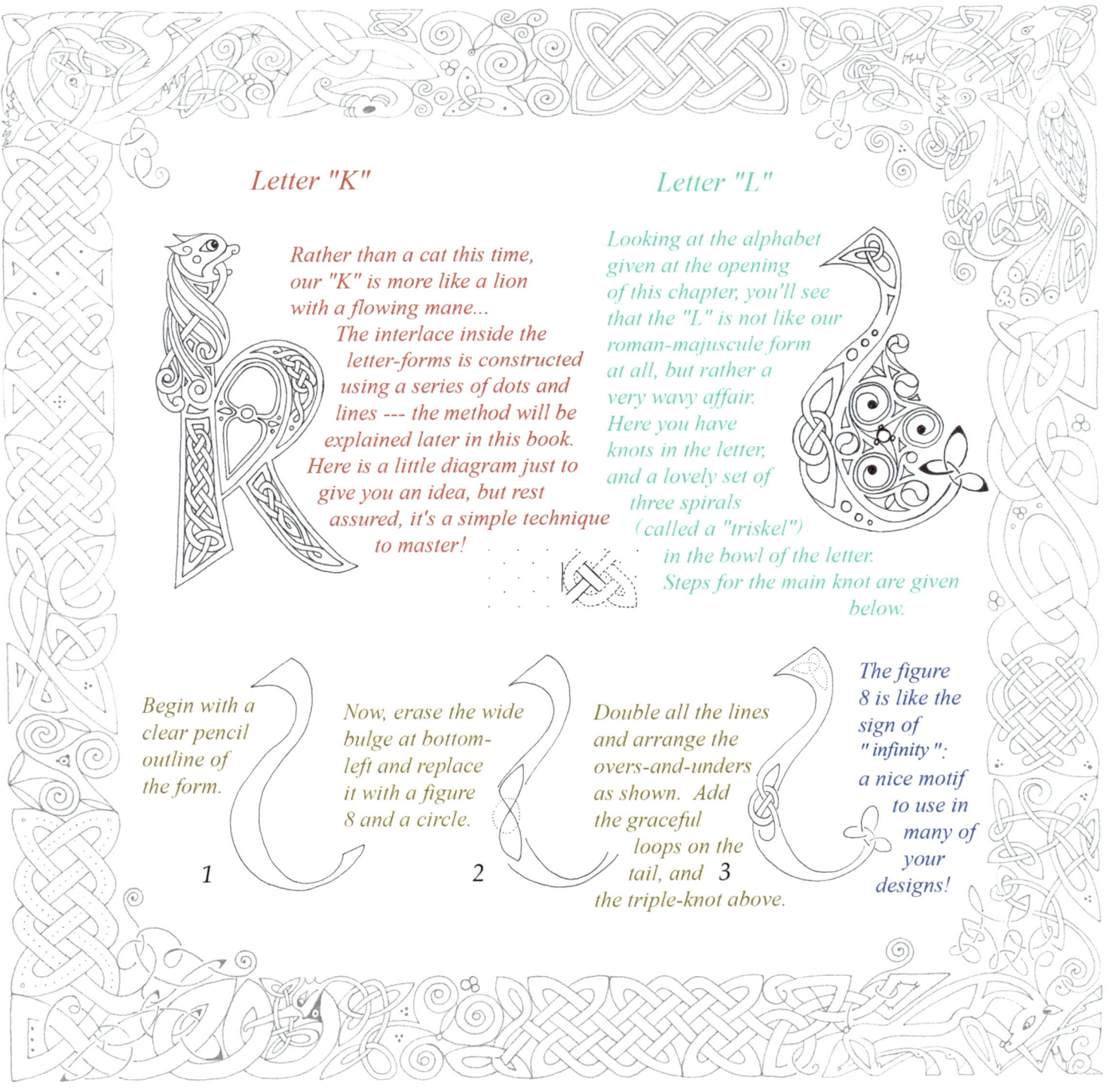

Letter "K"

Rather than a cat this time, our "K" is more like a lion with a flowing mane...
The interlace inside the letter-forms is constructed using a series of dots and lines --- the method will be explained later in this book. Here is a little diagram just to give you an idea, but rest assured, it's a simple technique to master!

Letter "L"

Looking at the alphabet given at the opening of this chapter, you'll see that the "L" is not like our roman-majuscule form at all, but rather a very wavy affair. Here you have knots in the letter, and a lovely set of three spirals (called a "triskel") in the bowl of the letter. Steps for the main knot are given below.

1 Begin with a clear pencil outline of the form.

2 Now, erase the wide bulge at bottom-left and replace it with a figure 8 and a circle.

3 Double all the lines and arrange the overs-and-unders as shown. Add the graceful loops on the tail, and the triple-knot above.

The figure 8 is like the sign of "infinity": a nice motif to use in many of your designs!

Letter "M"

This is a letter that shows the Celtic characteristic of variation in forms, even in regard to the two sides of the same letter! And a beard is always a good excuse for a tangle of interlace ...

1 2

3

Here you have the three steps for this decorative cross. Work in soft pencil and refine as you go, before doubling the cords...

Letter "N"

*Notice that the bar of the "N" is placed very low, **not** starting from the upper left. And that the left-leg of the letter descends much further than the right.*

At the two ends of the bar you find motifs called "step patterns", and inside the letter a very twisty animal... based on two loops and with just one hind leg!

Letter "O"

This curious form of "O" recalls the very ancient runic alphabets, much-loved by the Celtic scribes for titles and headings... The interior of this letter is filled with "key patterns". Below you have the steps to follow to create this lovely lozenge-motif.

1 2 3

... fill-in the spaces between the lines with black, but don't touch the "key" lines.

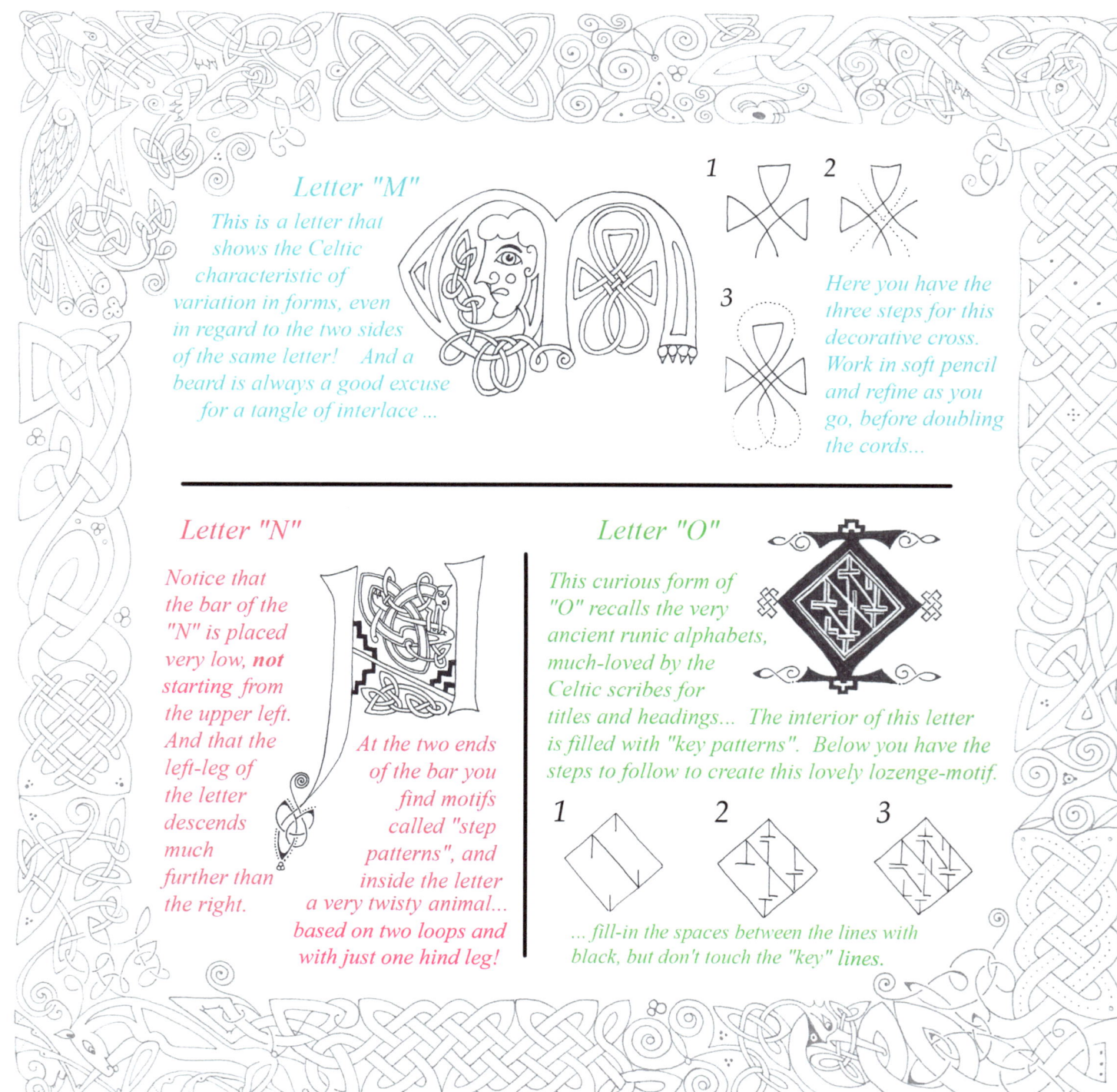

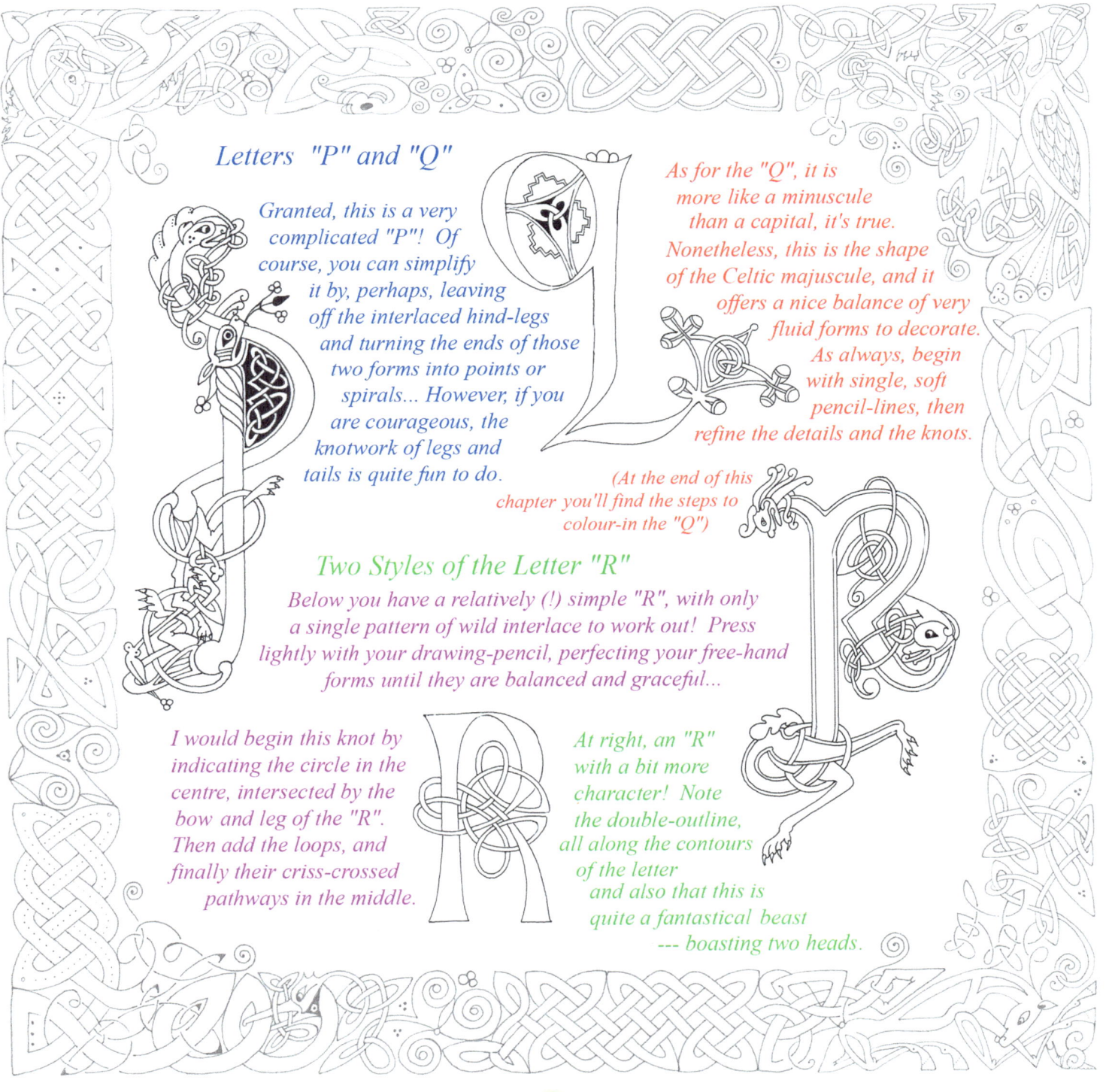

Letters "P" and "Q"

Granted, this is a very complicated "P"! Of course, you can simplify it by, perhaps, leaving off the interlaced hind-legs and turning the ends of those two forms into points or spirals... However, if you are courageous, the knotwork of legs and tails is quite fun to do.

As for the "Q", it is more like a minuscule than a capital, it's true. Nonetheless, this is the shape of the Celtic majuscule, and it offers a nice balance of very fluid forms to decorate. As always, begin with single, soft pencil-lines, then refine the details and the knots.

(At the end of this chapter you'll find the steps to colour-in the "Q")

Two Styles of the Letter "R"

Below you have a relatively (!) simple "R", with only a single pattern of wild interlace to work out! Press lightly with your drawing-pencil, perfecting your free-hand forms until they are balanced and graceful...

I would begin this knot by indicating the circle in the centre, intersected by the bow and leg of the "R". Then add the loops, and finally their criss-crossed pathways in the middle.

At right, an "R" with a bit more character! Note the double-outline, all along the contours of the letter and also that this is quite a fantastical beast --- boasting two heads.

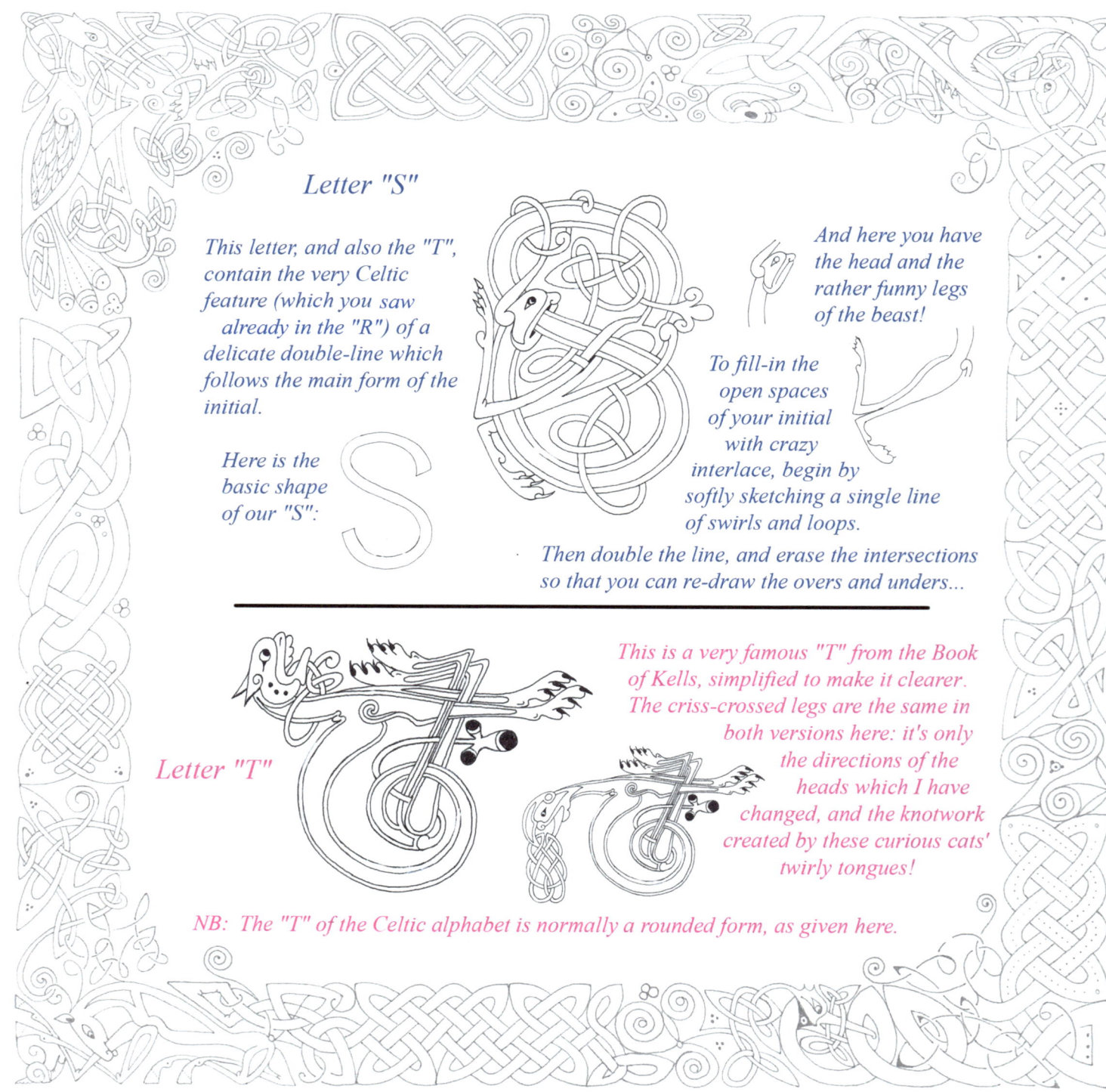

Letter "S"

This letter, and also the "T", contain the very Celtic feature (which you saw already in the "R") of a delicate double-line which follows the main form of the initial.

Here is the basic shape of our "S":

And here you have the head and the rather funny legs of the beast!

To fill-in the open spaces of your initial with crazy interlace, begin by softly sketching a single line of swirls and loops.

Then double the line, and erase the intersections so that you can re-draw the overs and unders...

Letter "T"

This is a very famous "T" from the Book of Kells, simplified to make it clearer. The criss-crossed legs are the same in both versions here: it's only the directions of the heads which I have changed, and the knotwork created by these curious cats' twirly tongues!

NB: The "T" of the Celtic alphabet is normally a rounded form, as given here.

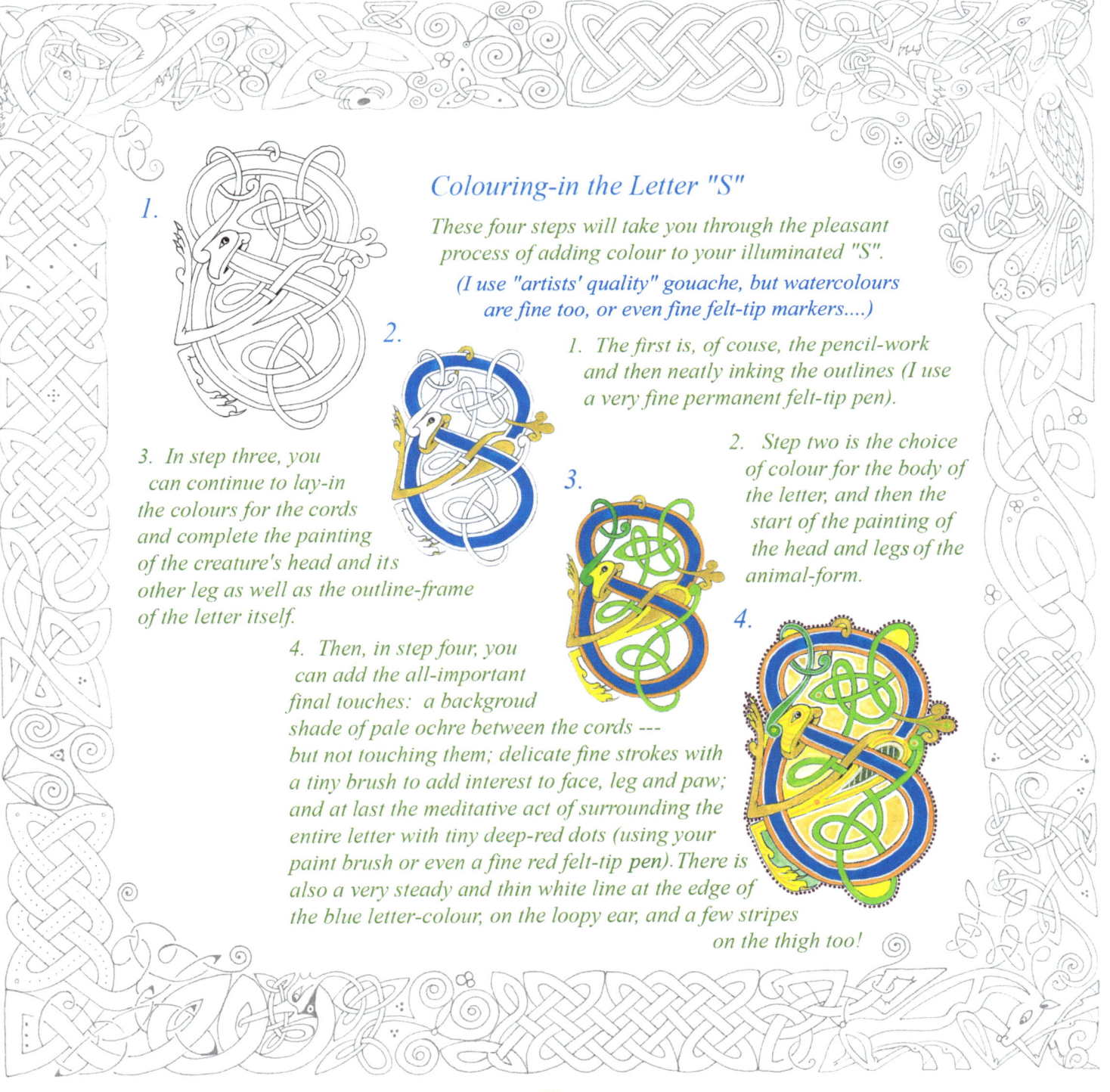

Colouring-in the Letter "S"

These four steps will take you through the pleasant process of adding colour to your illuminated "S".

(I use "artists' quality" gouache, but watercolours are fine too, or even fine felt-tip markers....)

1. The first is, of couse, the pencil-work and then neatly inking the outlines (I use a very fine permanent felt-tip pen).

2. Step two is the choice of colour for the body of the letter, and then the start of the painting of the head and legs of the animal-form.

3. In step three, you can continue to lay-in the colours for the cords and complete the painting of the creature's head and its other leg as well as the outline-frame of the letter itself.

4. Then, in step four, you can add the all-important final touches: a backgroud shade of pale ochre between the cords --- but not touching them; delicate fine strokes with a tiny brush to add interest to face, leg and paw; and at last the meditative act of surrounding the entire letter with tiny deep-red dots (using your paint brush or even a fine red felt-tip *pen*). There is also a very steady and thin white line at the edge of the blue letter-colour, on the loopy ear, and a few stripes on the thigh too!

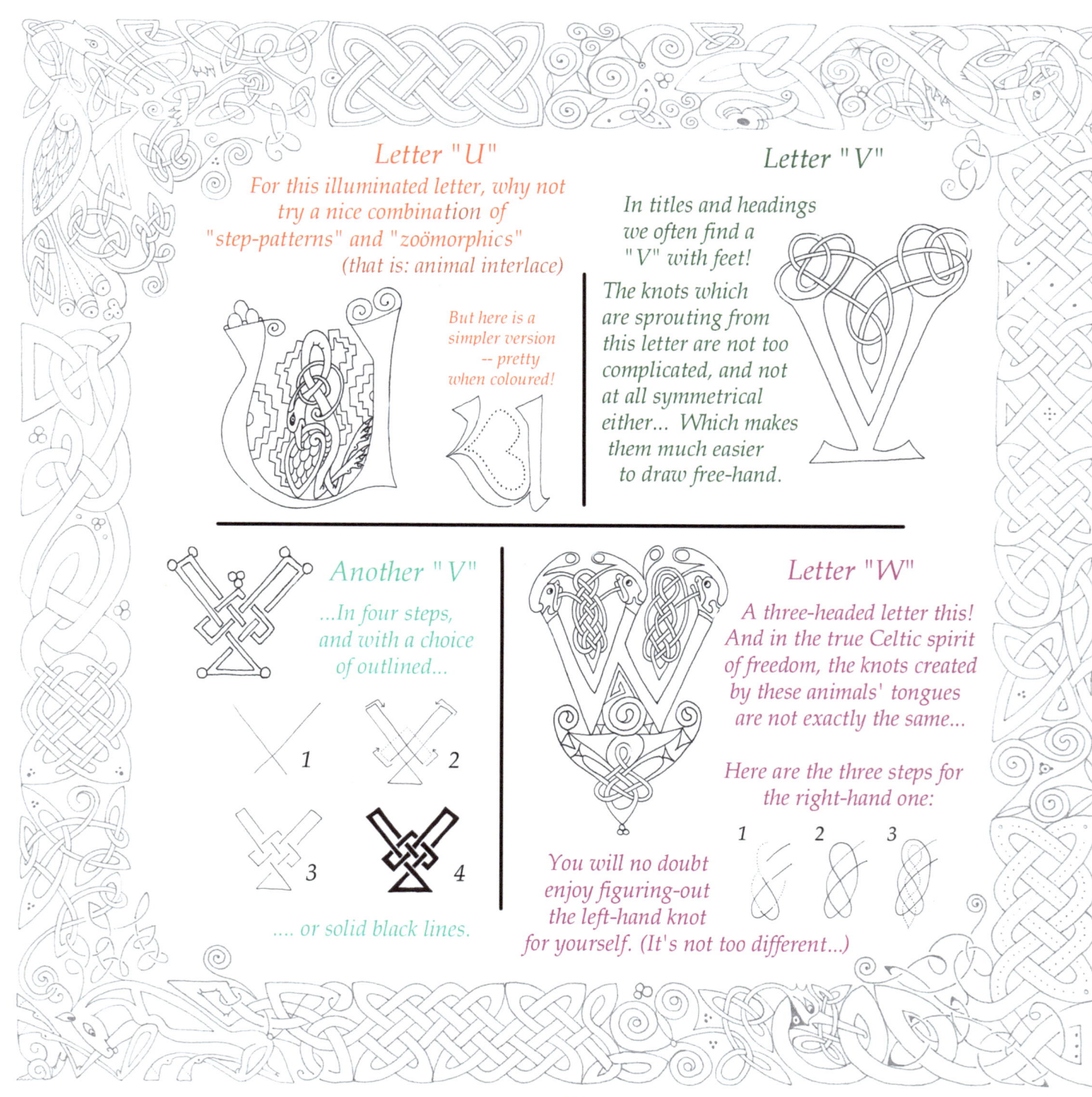

Letter "U"

For this illuminated letter, why not try a nice combination of "step-patterns" and "zoömorphics" (that is: animal interlace)

But here is a simpler version -- pretty when coloured!

Letter "V"

In titles and headings we often find a "V" with feet!

The knots which are sprouting from this letter are not too complicated, and not at all symmetrical either... Which makes them much easier to draw free-hand.

Another "V"

...In four steps, and with a choice of outlined...

.... or solid black lines.

Letter "W"

A three-headed letter this! And in the true Celtic spirit of freedom, the knots created by these animals' tongues are not exactly the same...

Here are the three steps for the right-hand one:

You will no doubt enjoy figuring-out the left-hand knot for yourself. (It's not too different...)

Illuminating the Letter "W"

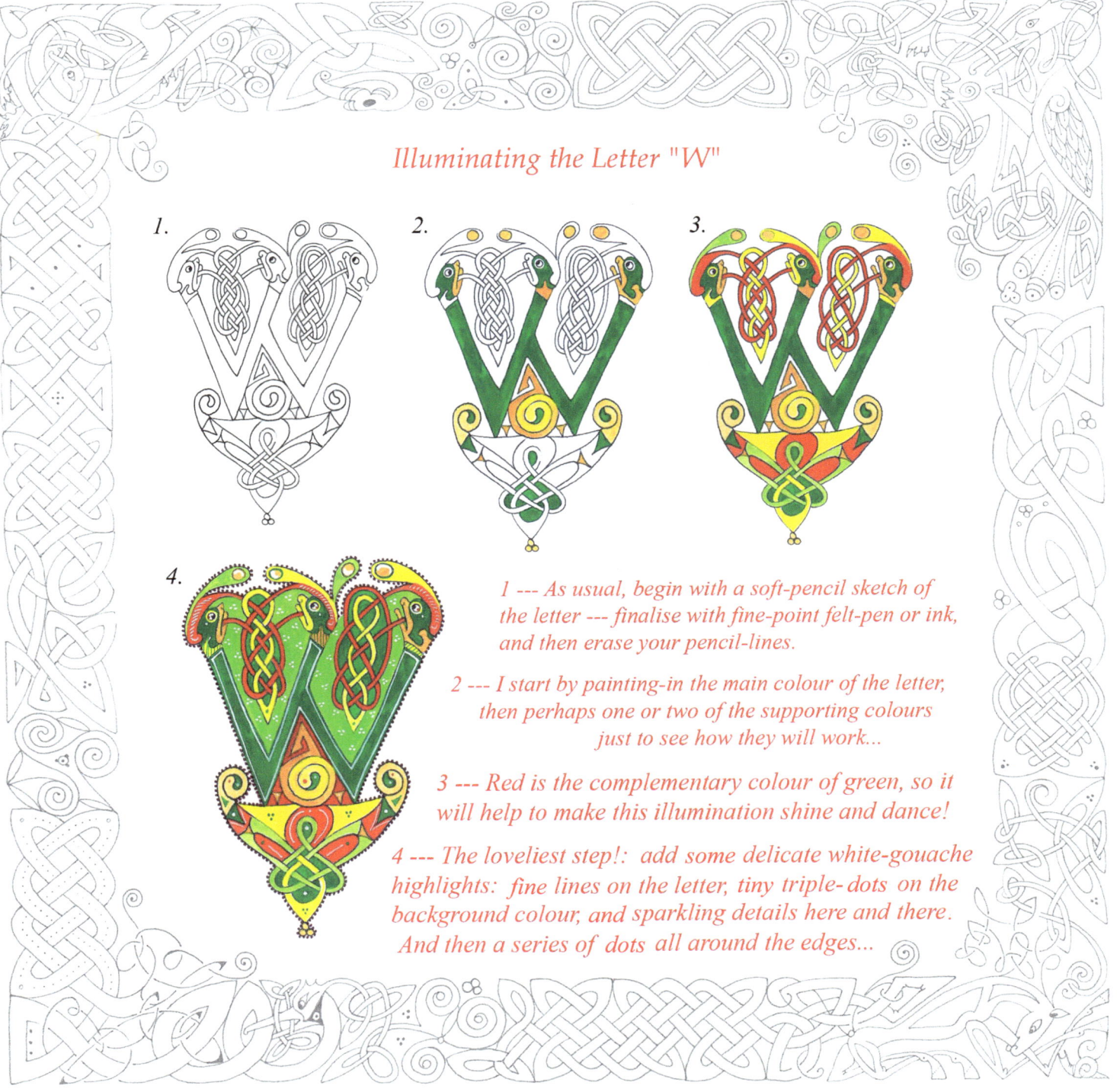

1 --- As usual, begin with a soft-pencil sketch of the letter --- finalise with fine-point felt-pen or ink, and then erase your pencil-lines.

2 --- I start by painting-in the main colour of the letter, then perhaps one or two of the supporting colours just to see how they will work...

3 --- Red is the complementary colour of green, so it will help to make this illumination shine and dance!

4 --- The loveliest step!: add some delicate white-gouache highlights: fine lines on the letter, tiny triple-dots on the background colour, and sparkling details here and there. And then a series of dots all around the edges...

Letters "X", "Y" and "Z"

The "X" is a very graceful letter in Celtic. Here we leave it quite plain and clear, with just a couple of spirals...

... and an airy knot at the end of its long leg, like a side-ways heart.

The true "Y" of our alphabet is very strange! In the example below, I've given it a dragon-head, and a few looping knots.

This invented one is perhaps more "y"-like, but more demanding, it's true.

And how could we ignore the famous "Z" of the Gospel Prefaces from the Book of Kells, with its cats chasing around it?! All of its compartments are filled with interlace, or zoömorphics, or tiny triangle-patterns... each one framed by a border. The form of the letter is very original too, with its curling tail --- nicely echoed in the spiral of the tail of the lower cat... A real "tour de force"!

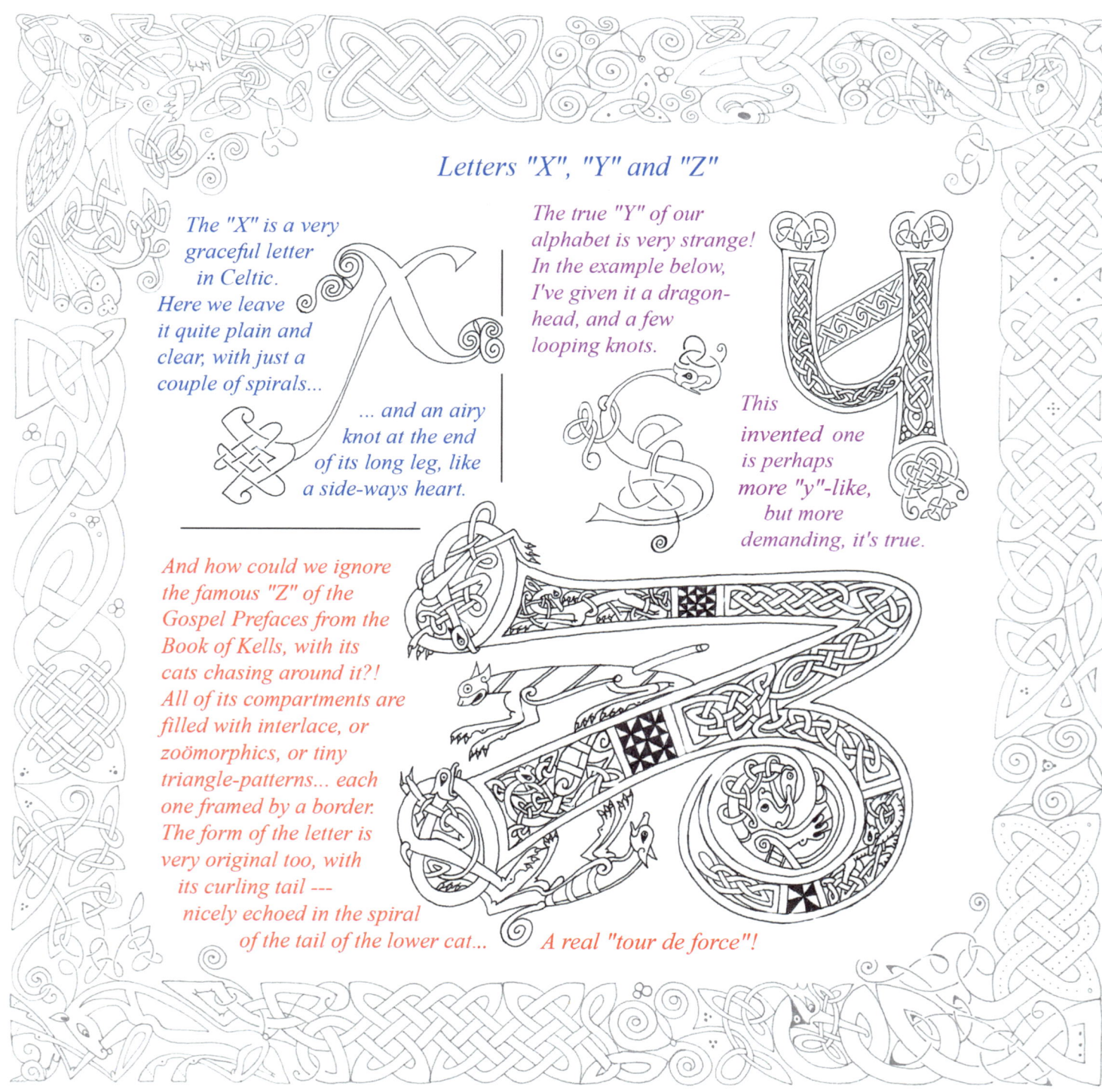

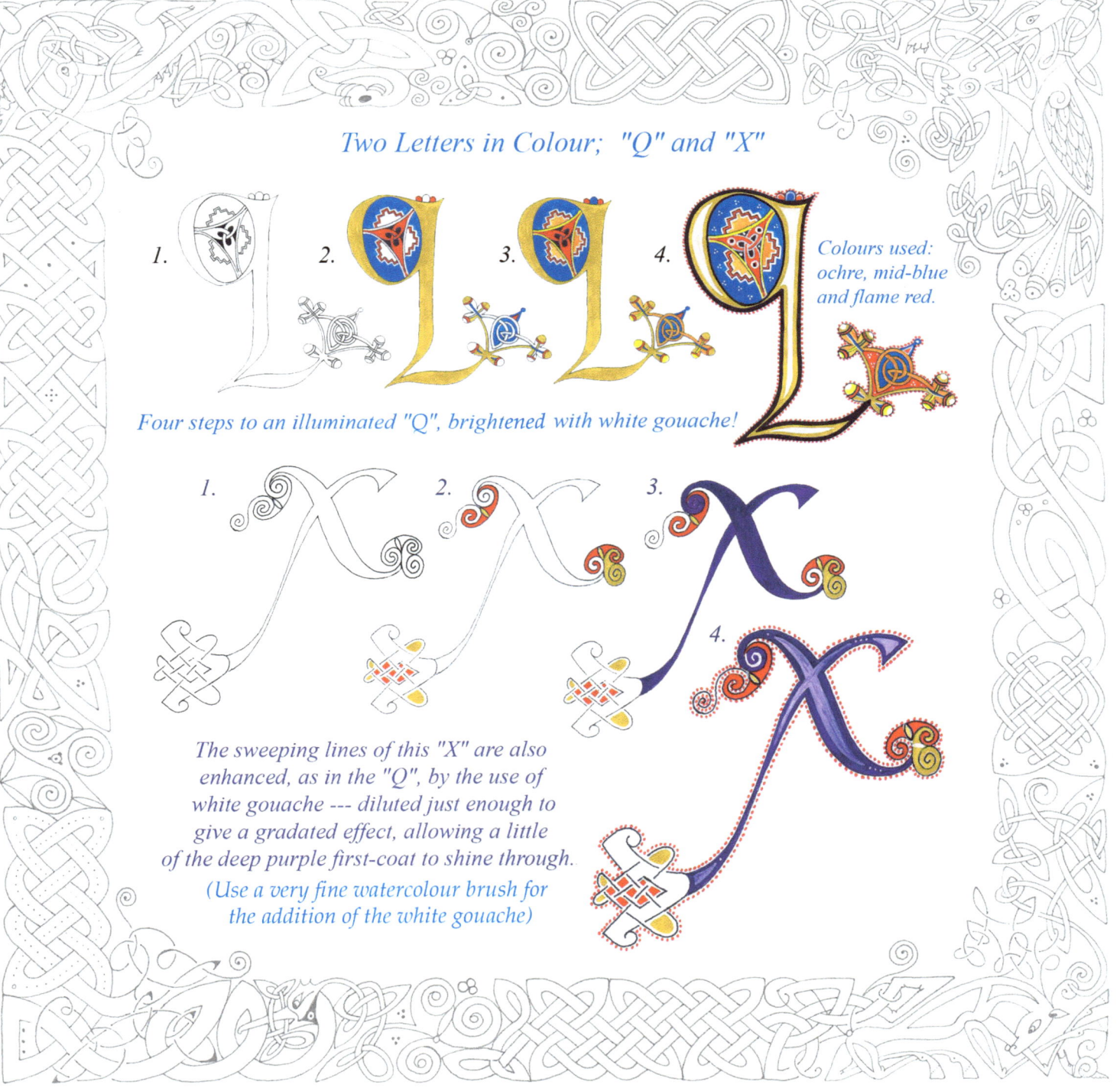

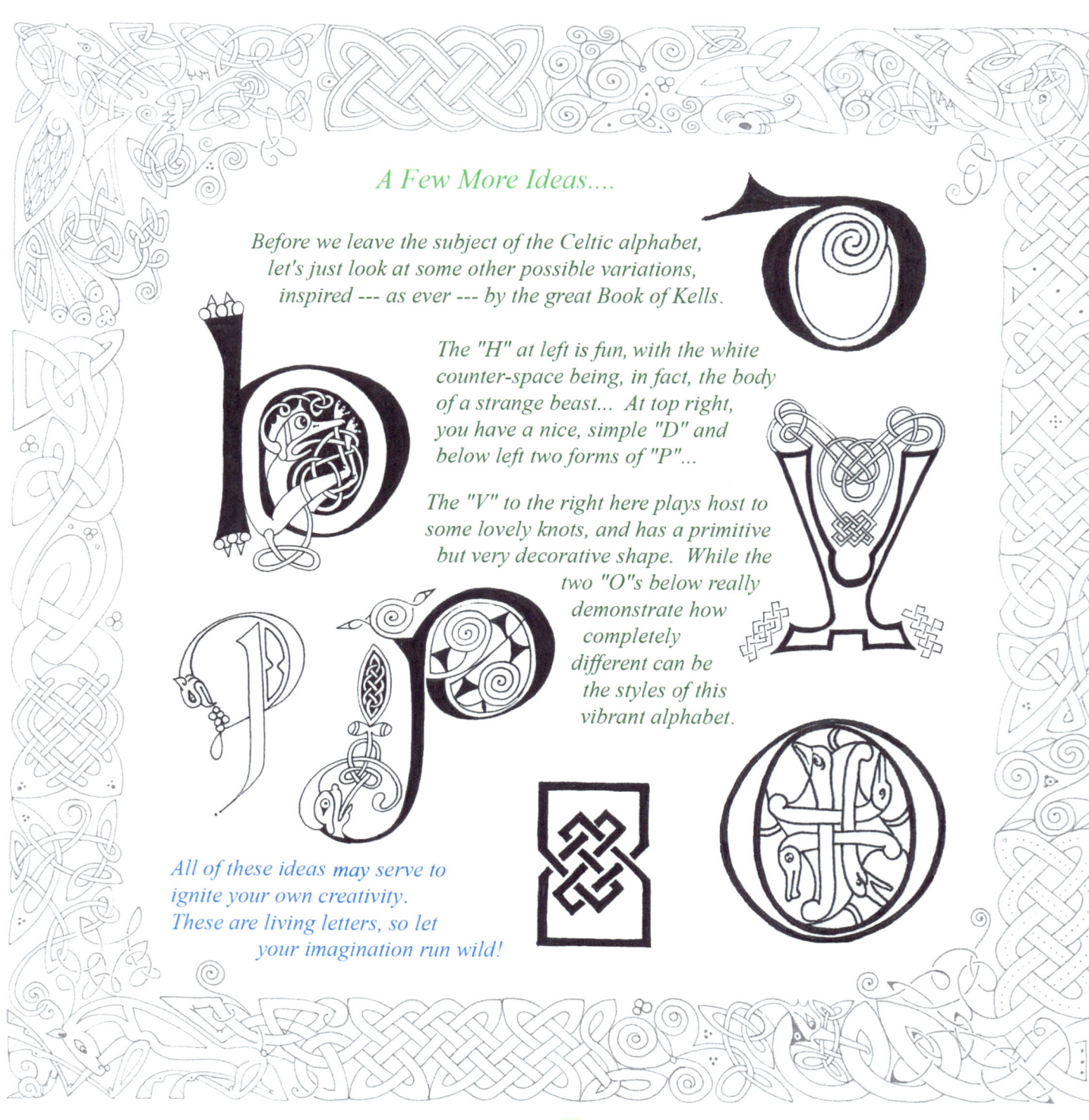

A Few More Ideas....

Before we leave the subject of the Celtic alphabet, let's just look at some other possible variations, inspired --- as ever --- by the great Book of Kells.

The "H" at left is fun, with the white counter-space being, in fact, the body of a strange beast... At top right, you have a nice, simple "D" and below left two forms of "P"...

The "V" to the right here plays host to some lovely knots, and has a primitive but very decorative shape. While the two "O"s below really demonstrate how completely different can be the styles of this vibrant alphabet.

All of these ideas may serve to ignite your own creativity. These are living letters, so let your imagination run wild!

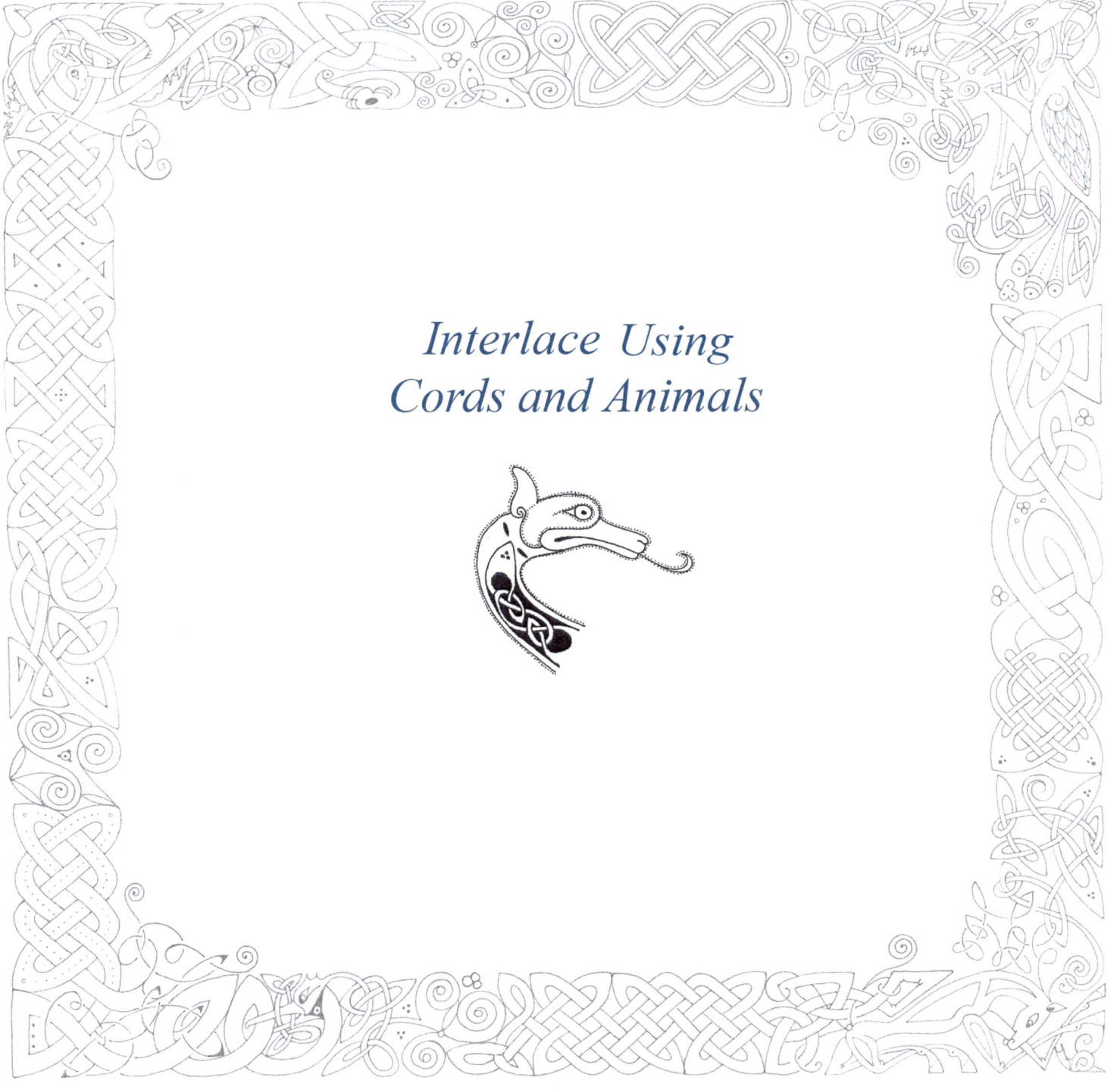

Interlace Using Cords and Animals

Interlace Panels, Using Guide-Dots

This is a delightfully simple way to construct endless variations of knotwork. In step 1 you draw a series of equidistant dots (here in blue), then add dots (in red here) in the centre of each square of blue dots. Now, imagine that <u>pathways</u> can go along the diagonals between groups of dots: two blue and two red, but adjacent paths always go in <u>opposite</u> diagonals, and at the corners or walls they turn back on themselves (step 2).

In step 3 you see how the overs and unders take shape of their own accord, just by alternating the diagonal pathways. In step 4 you can imagine adding colours, and where the blue and red dots are visible between the cords, you can fill-in with black --- or erase the dots.

1. 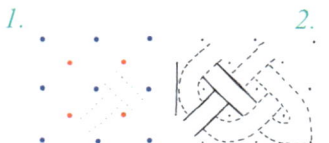 *2.* 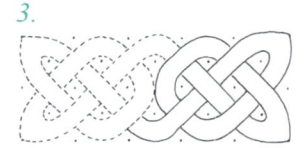 *3.*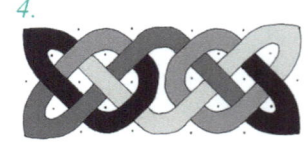

Theme and Variations!:

You can make your panels as long or as thick as you like with this method --- with a minimum of three blue points in any direction.
By adding "walls" between certain points, you create the interior turns and breaks in the knots.

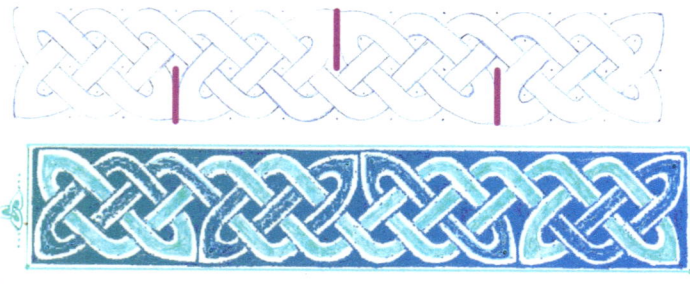

Traditionally the background is coloured-in darker than the cords, and there is often a framework running along each cord also, here in white... but it could be in a contrasting colour too.

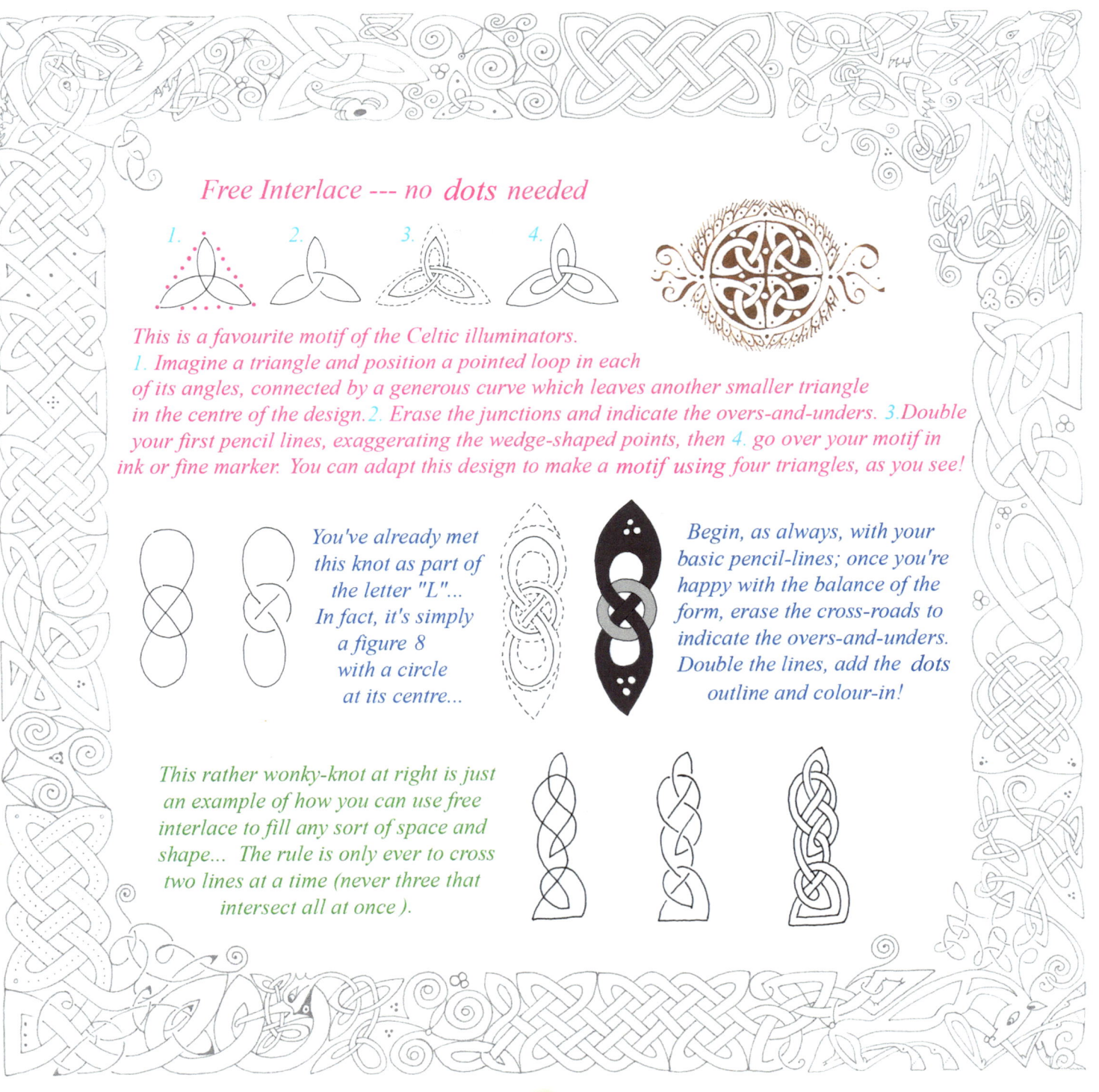

Free Interlace --- no dots needed

This is a favourite motif of the Celtic illuminators.
1. Imagine a triangle and position a pointed loop in each of its angles, connected by a generous curve which leaves another smaller triangle in the centre of the design. 2. Erase the junctions and indicate the overs-and-unders. 3. Double your first pencil lines, exaggerating the wedge-shaped points, then 4. go over your motif in ink or fine marker. You can adapt this design to make a *motif using four triangles*, as you see!

You've already met this knot as part of the letter "L"... In fact, it's simply a figure 8 with a circle at its centre...

Begin, as always, with your basic pencil-lines; once you're happy with the balance of the form, erase the cross-roads to indicate the overs-and-unders. Double the lines, add the *dots* outline and colour-in!

This rather wonky-knot at right is just an example of how you can use free interlace to fill any sort of space and shape... The rule is only ever to cross two lines at a time (never three that intersect all at once).

Other Rounded and Geometric Knots

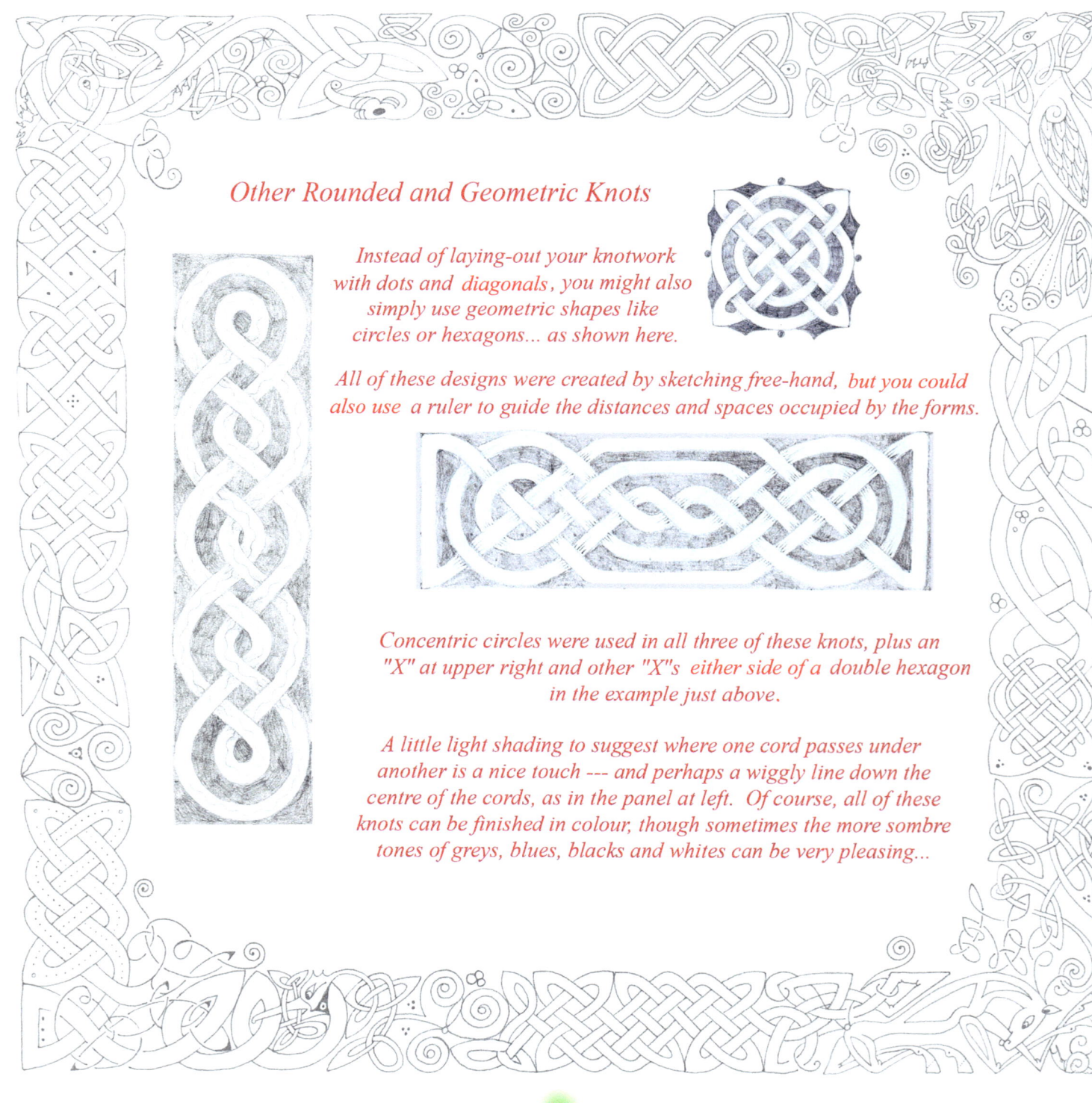

Instead of laying-out your knotwork with dots and diagonals, you might also simply use geometric shapes like circles or hexagons... as shown here.

All of these designs were created by sketching free-hand, but you could also use a ruler to guide the distances and spaces occupied by the forms.

Concentric circles were used in all three of these knots, plus an "X" at upper right and other "X"s either side of a double hexagon in the example just above.

A little light shading to suggest where one cord passes under another is a nice touch --- and perhaps a wiggly line down the centre of the cords, as in the panel at left. Of course, all of these knots can be finished in colour, though sometimes the more sombre tones of greys, blues, blacks and whites can be very pleasing...

Snail-Knots

My name for this type of interlace panel is <u>not</u> meant to invoke the pace at which you work! It's just that I find the forms remind me of snail-shells...

Begin with these three rows of dots --- in a panel that can be upright or sideways: evenly spaced black dots, and green ones at the centres of each "square" formed by the first two rows.

Now, draw the short diagonal lines in every <u>second</u> lozenge-shape, as above. Remember not to go beyond the four points, two black and two green, of each "lozenge"...

Ether side of these first lines, draw two more diagonals to make "X"s, then a half-circle to the lower left of each "X" and a quarter-circle to link-up with the top-right arm of each.

Finally, add the upper and lower arches, as above.

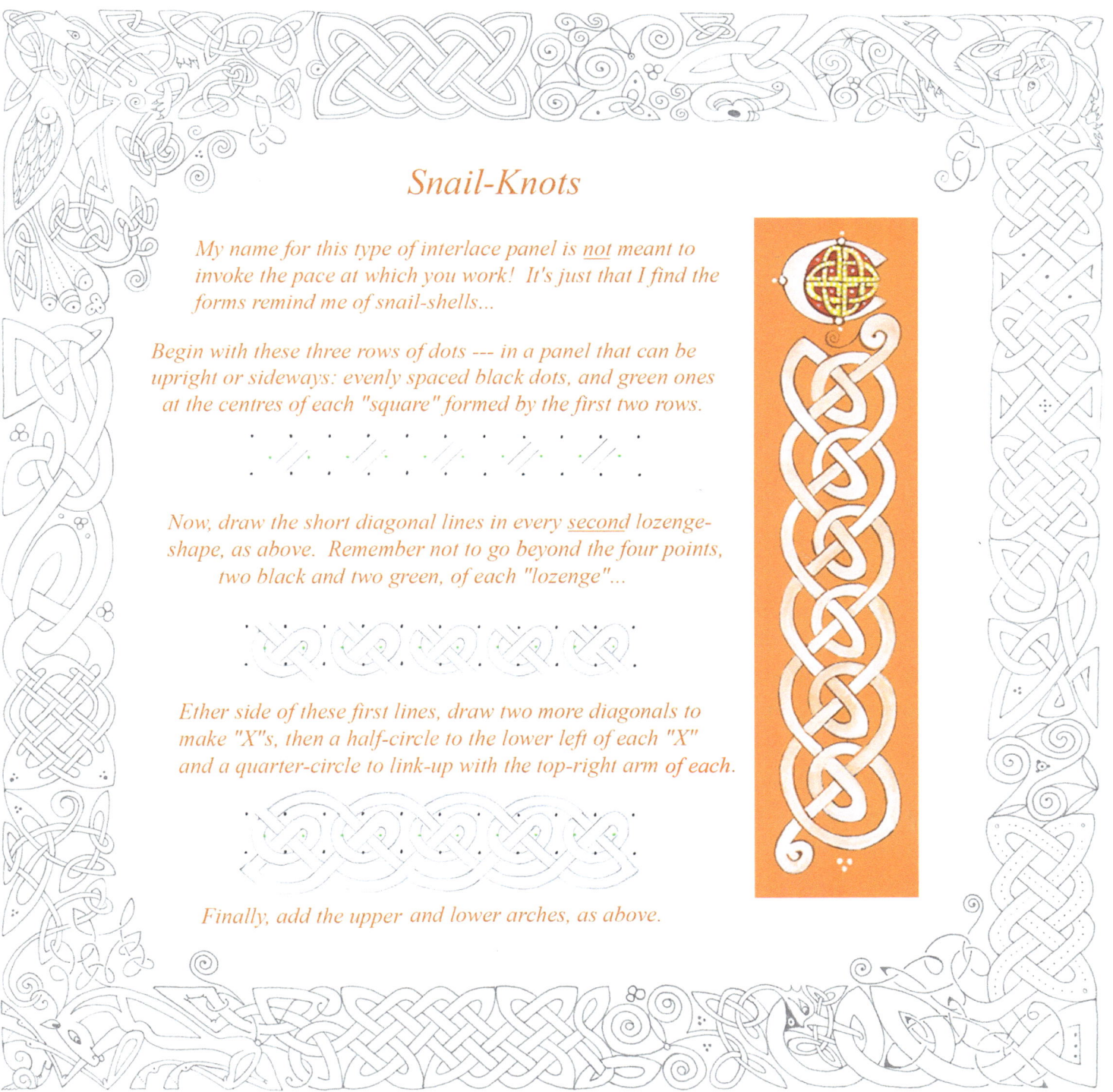

Just to Complicate Things a Bit!

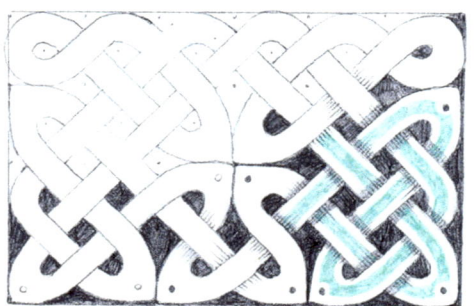

This panel, to the left, is created using our series of dots - but with numerous breaks or "walls" to add turns and twists to the road!

The first step could be to lightly sketch all of the diagonals without ANY walls, and then to add them one at a time, erasing and redrawing the turns as you go... The underlying woven knotwork remains the same in any case.

To the right is an invitation to take your interlace to another level! Begin with normal cords, in soft pencil-line, and then divide each cord in <u>three parts</u>: two thin arms and a central space of the same width. At each intersection you will now need to redraw the overs-and-unders so that each of the four "arms" make a criss-cross...
(always in the same order, by the way). Endless fun!

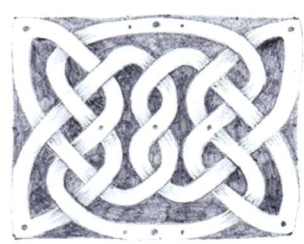

And this little motif is also made using a grid of dots, but at top and bottom allowing the cords to "leap" over several dots and reconnect in a soft arch. The use of a grid of dots gives you a foundation for creating many, many variations, and keeps the overs-and-unders clear to the eye.

An Interlace "Mandala"

The method for doing circular knotwork is the same as that you have seen for rectangular spaces. The only difference is that you must "bend" your series of dots (in both colours) and space them out evenly around the circle.

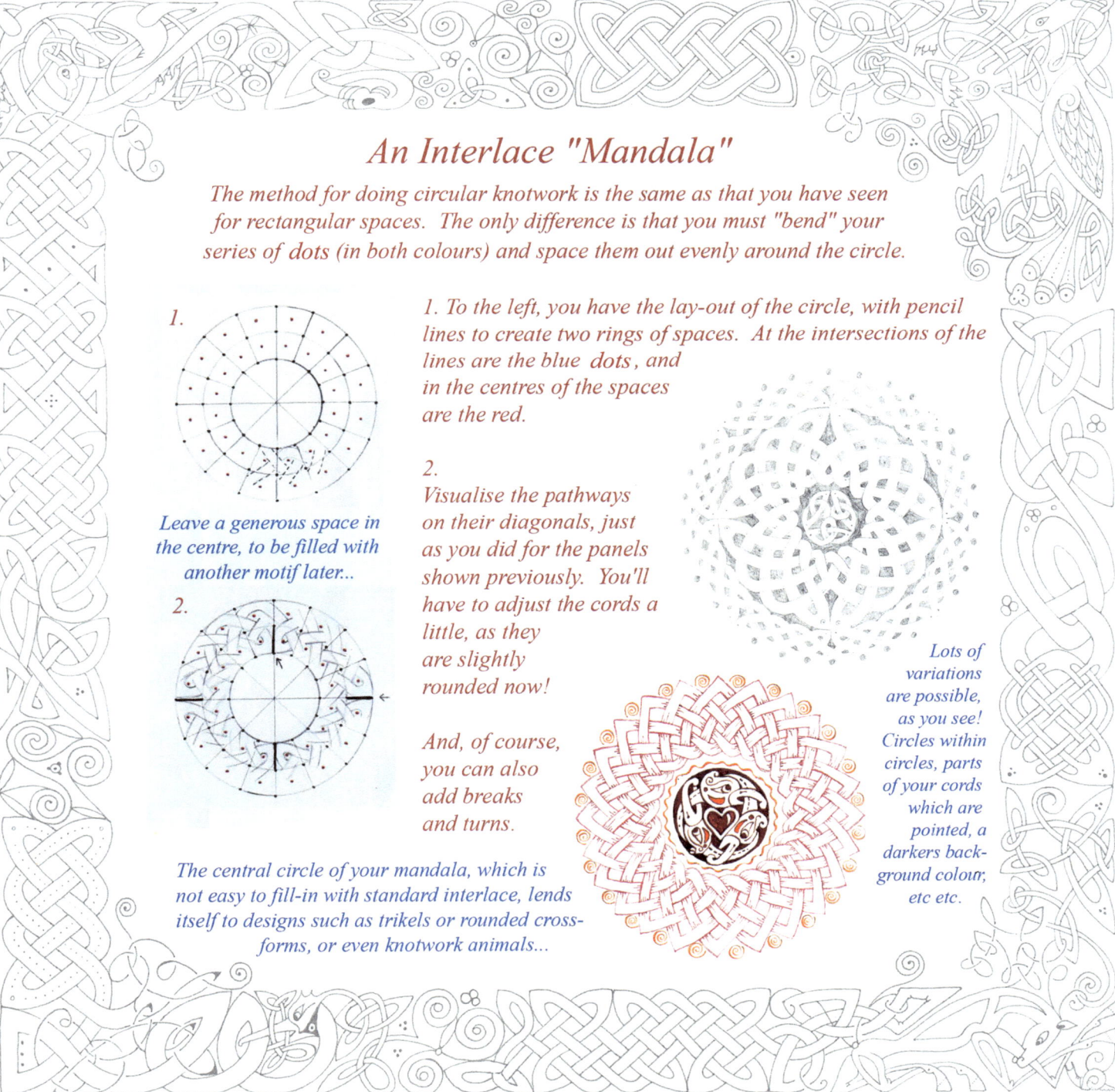

1.

Leave a generous space in the centre, to be filled with another motif later...

2.

1. To the left, you have the lay-out of the circle, with pencil lines to create two rings of spaces. At the intersections of the lines are the blue *dots*, and in the centres of the spaces are the red.

2. Visualise the pathways on their diagonals, just as you did for the panels shown previously. You'll have to adjust the cords a little, as they are slightly rounded now!

And, of course, you can also add breaks and turns.

Lots of variations are possible, as you see! Circles within circles, parts of your cords which are pointed, a darkers background colour, etc etc.

The central circle of your mandala, which is not easy to fill-in with standard interlace, lends itself to designs such as trikels or rounded cross-forms, or even knotwork animals...

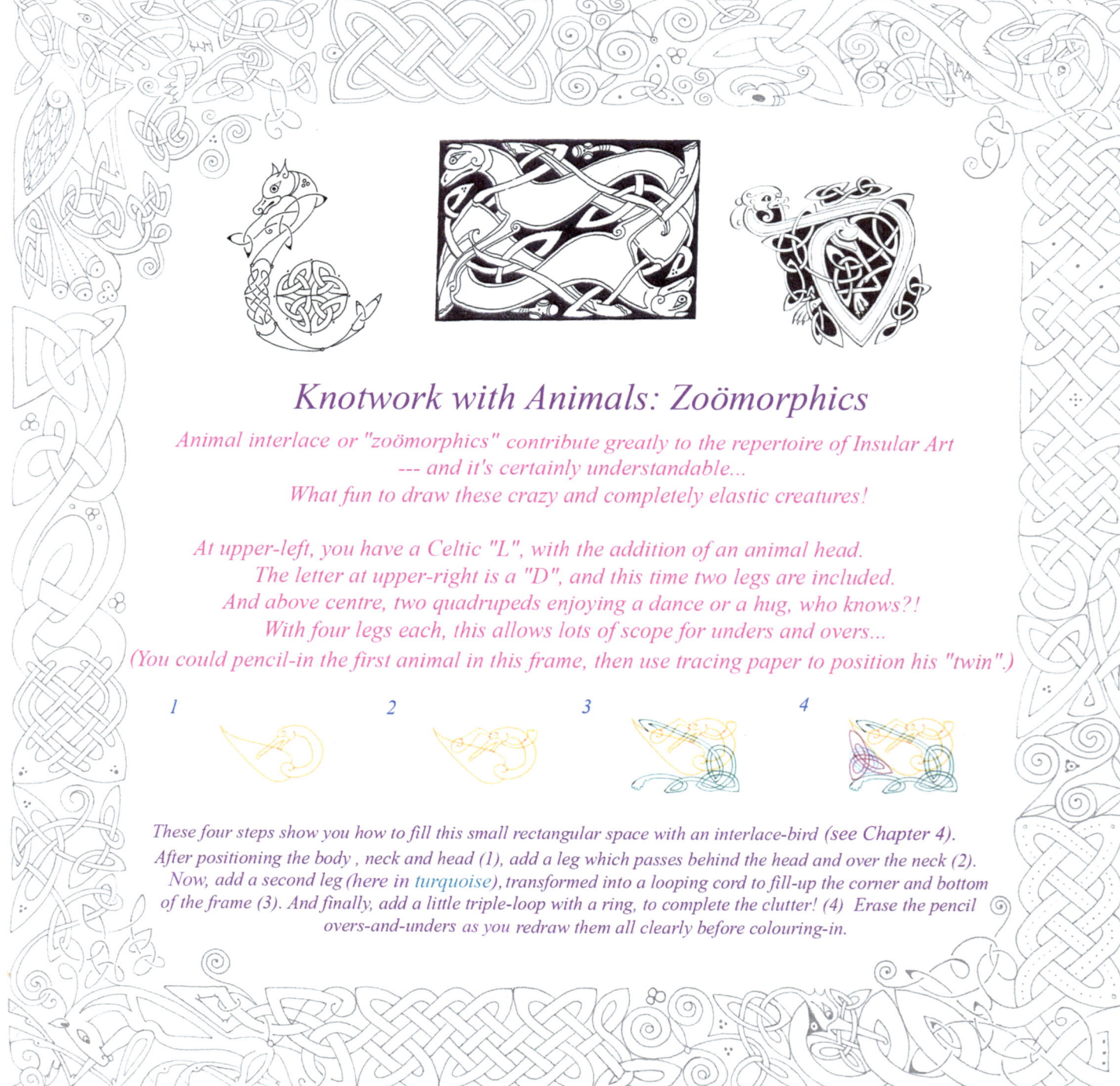

Knotwork with Animals: Zoömorphics

Animal interlace or "zoömorphics" contribute greatly to the repertoire of Insular Art
--- and it's certainly understandable...
What fun to draw these crazy and completely elastic creatures!

At upper-left, you have a Celtic "L", with the addition of an animal head.
The letter at upper-right is a "D", and this time two legs are included.
And above centre, two quadrupeds enjoying a dance or a hug, who knows?!
With four legs each, this allows lots of scope for unders and overs...
(You could pencil-in the first animal in this frame, then use tracing paper to position his "twin".)

1   2   3   4

These four steps show you how to fill this small rectangular space with an interlace-bird (see Chapter 4). After positioning the body, neck and head (1), add a leg which passes behind the head and over the neck (2). Now, add a second leg (here in turquoise), transformed into a looping cord to fill-up the corner and bottom of the frame (3). And finally, add a little triple-loop with a ring, to complete the clutter! (4) Erase the pencil overs-and-unders as you redraw them all clearly before colouring-in.

The Many Faces of Zoömorphics

Luckily, almost ALL the animals in Celtic art have heads and faces based on the same forms. Be they cats or dogs, birds or more exotic beasts, all share a rounded eye-shape, with a little triangle behind it, a rather S-shaped head and then a mouth to go with their species. By varying only one or two details, you change the creature!

At right, six steps for drawing the basic shape of the eye, the forehead, the mouth and the pointed ear.

At lower-right, this "D" sports a nice animal-head, with knots occuring in neck and body --- the latter ending in a swirling triskel motif.

The heads above might give you more ideas for decoration: an ear ending in a cord long enough to pass through the mouth, a line very delicately doubled, a knot inside the neck (swallowed by mistake?!), or an original form growing out from the back of the head...

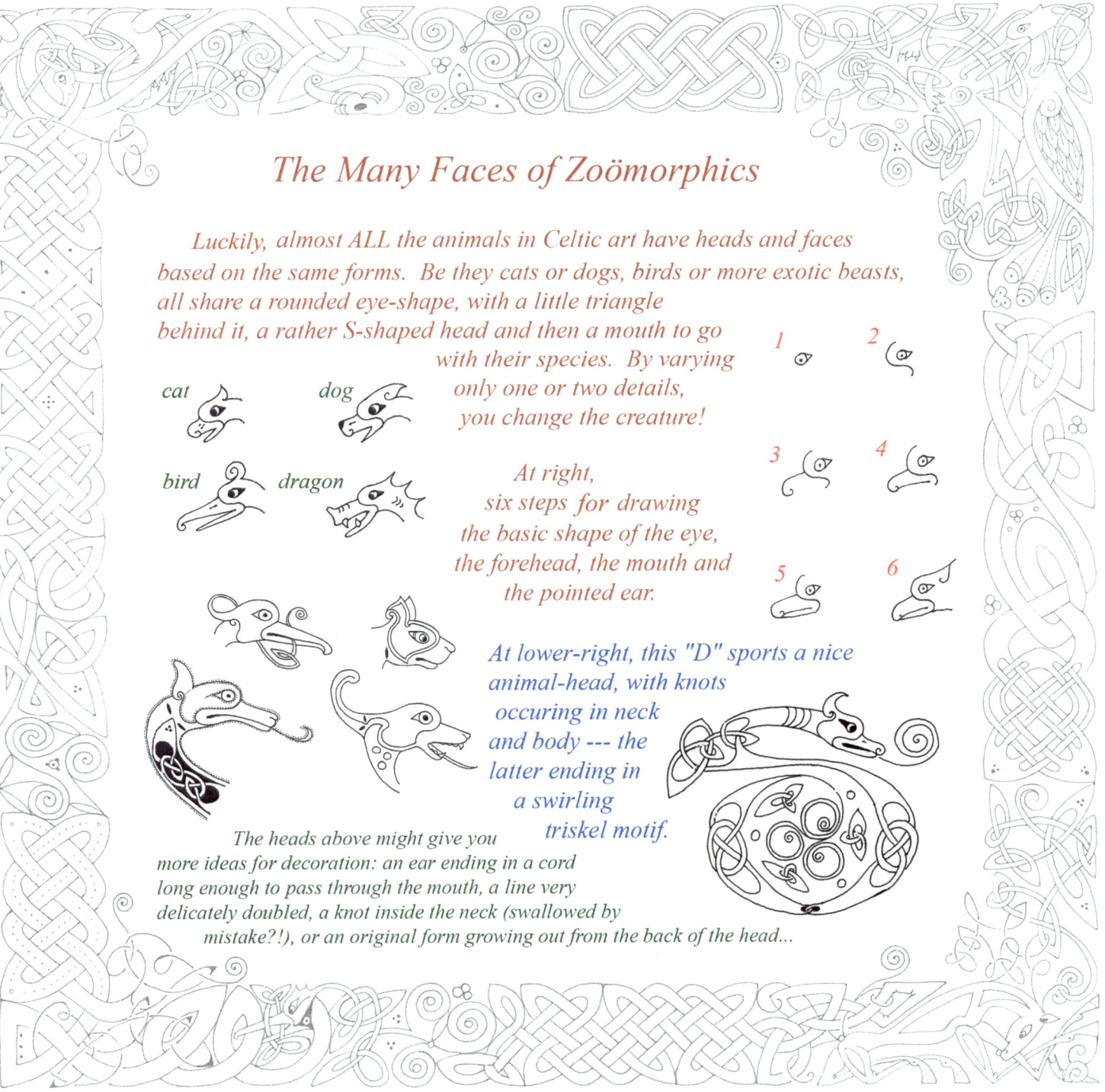

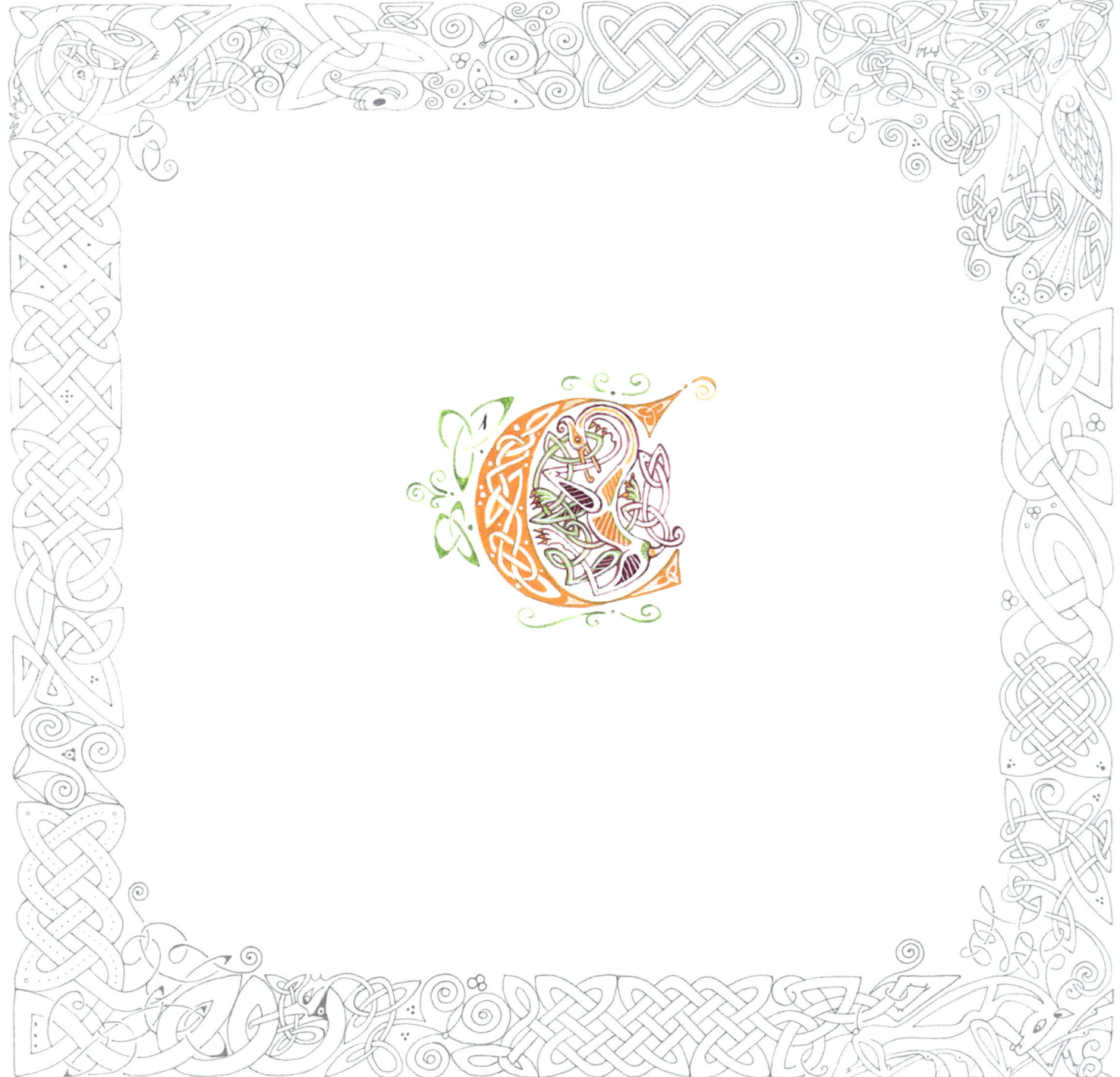

Monograms

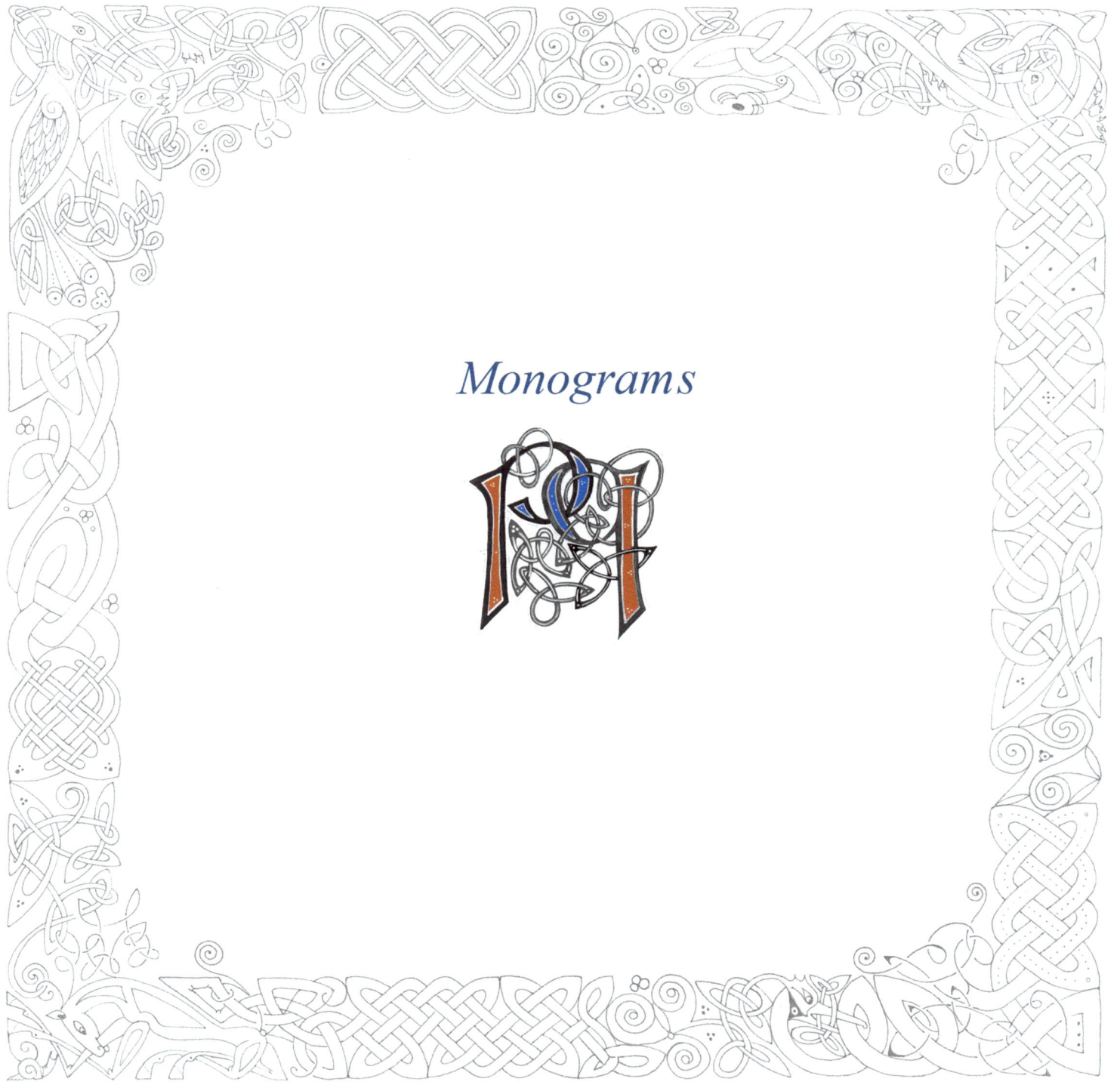

A Simple Little Monogram

Well, perhaps not **too** simple! But, at least for the first step of drawing the shapes of the two letters, all is clear and straight-forward. Once the "J" and "P" are in place, the fun begins!

The free-form interlace which fills all the background of this monogram is done in very soft pencil, really as if doodling! Be prepared to try many ideas, to erase, and to modify. Keep the loops soft and fluid.

The first step in the decoration, for me, is to add the heads of both letters. Here you see the bird-like heads I've put at the end of the J's lower loop and on the curling interior form of the P.

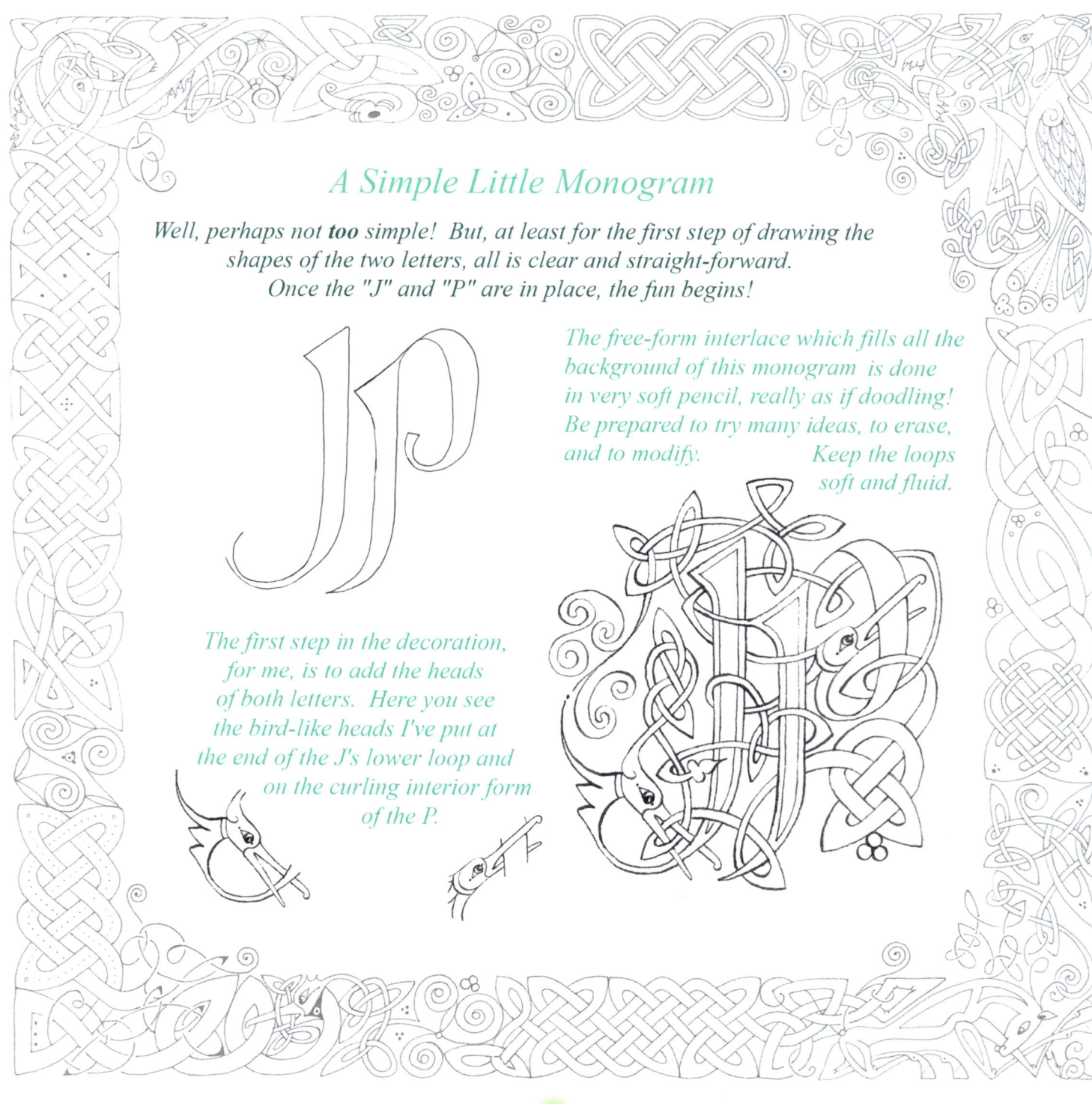

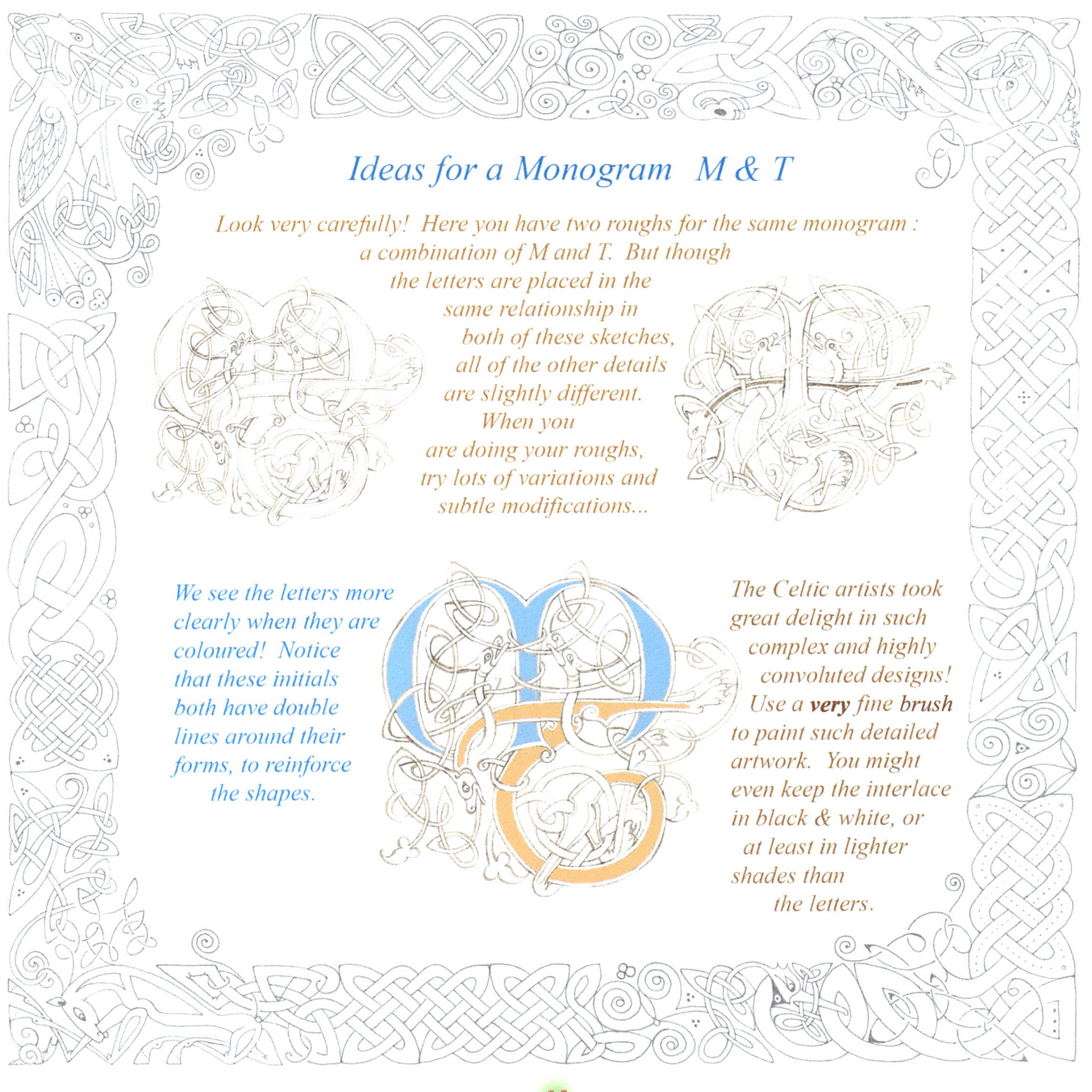

Ideas for a Monogram   M & T

Look very carefully! Here you have two roughs for the same monogram : a combination of M and T. But though the letters are placed in the same relationship in both of these sketches, all of the other details are slightly different. When you are doing your roughs, try lots of variations and subtle modifications...

We see the letters more clearly when they are coloured! Notice that these initials both have double lines around their forms, to reinforce the shapes.

The Celtic artists took great delight in such complex and highly convoluted designs! Use a **very** fine brush to paint such detailed artwork. You might even keep the interlace in black & white, or at least in lighter shades than the letters.

Various Monograms

These two designs, in black & white, explore the possibilities for combining E & K (or K & E!). Free interlace or knots made using points, spirals and zoömorphics... Such elements could find their way into many of your own creations!

The monogram at right combines J and E. The client for this project asked for some rather "un-Celtic" motifs --- but fun to include: a wild boar, some flowers and a ship! The central area of each letter was embellished with real gold leaf.

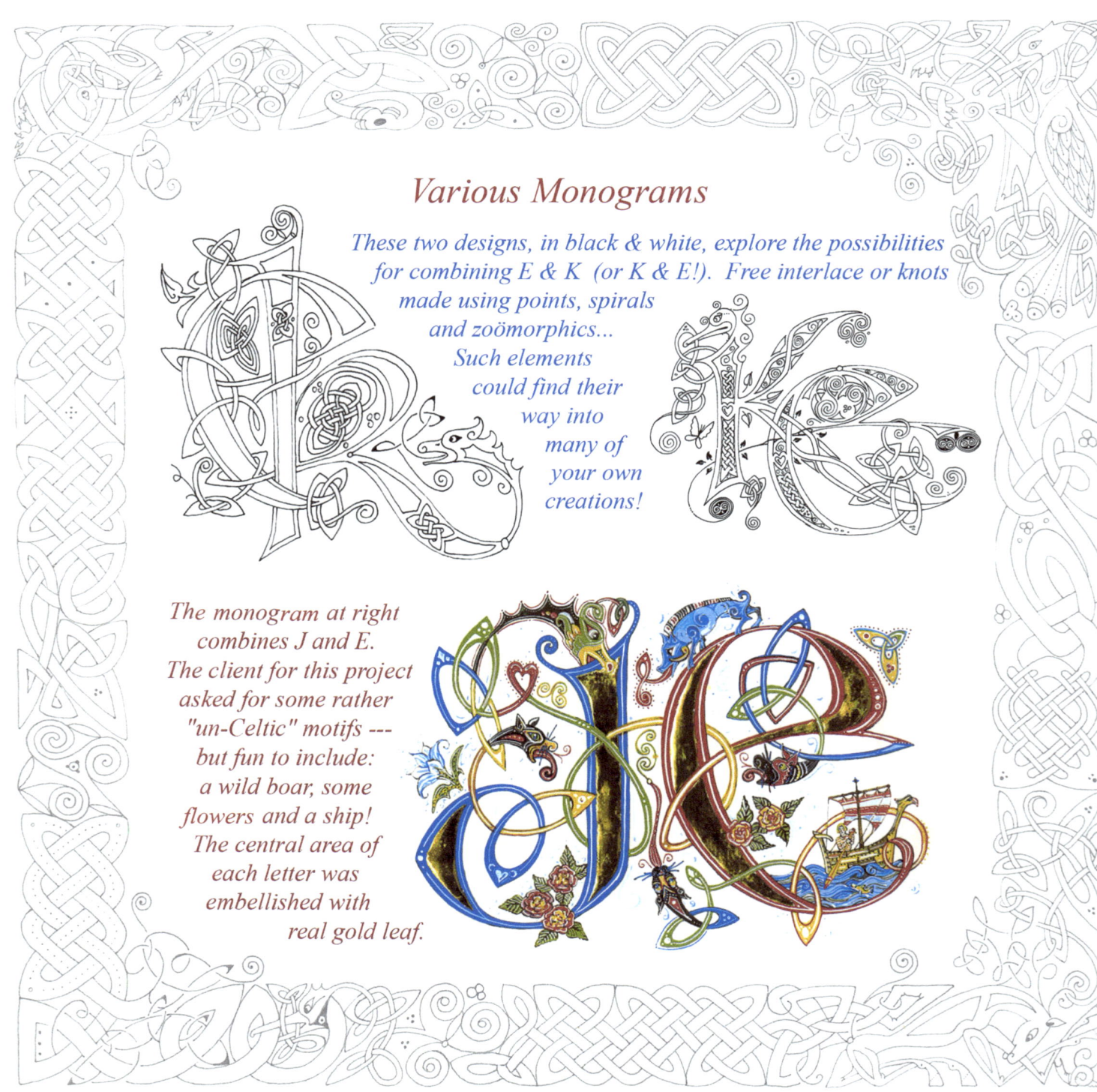

Three Monograms K & E

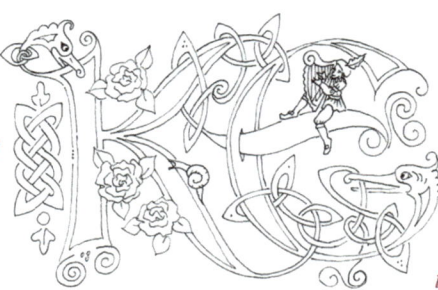

Here's another project where some not-too-Celtic designs were used! Stylised roses, a little musician, and even a friendly snail...

It's always amusing to try lots of composition ideas, allowing your imagination to run riot. In fact, you often find that the letters are so alive that they seem to have ideas of their own...

In this final, colour version, I truly made a hybrid-design, with Celtic knots and letter-forms mixed with leaves and flowers, even in the white-gouache details painted onto the body-colours of the letters.

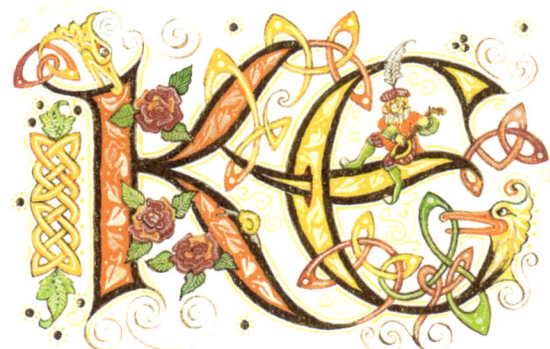

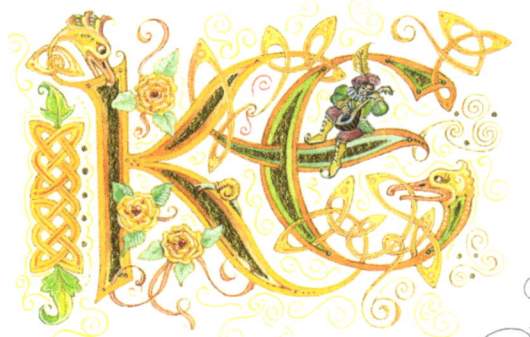

And the example at right is just as multi-styled. The gold of the central spaces of each letter is not gold-leaf, but rather a powered metallic gouache. And diluted watercolours are used on the leaves (softer than opaque gouache).

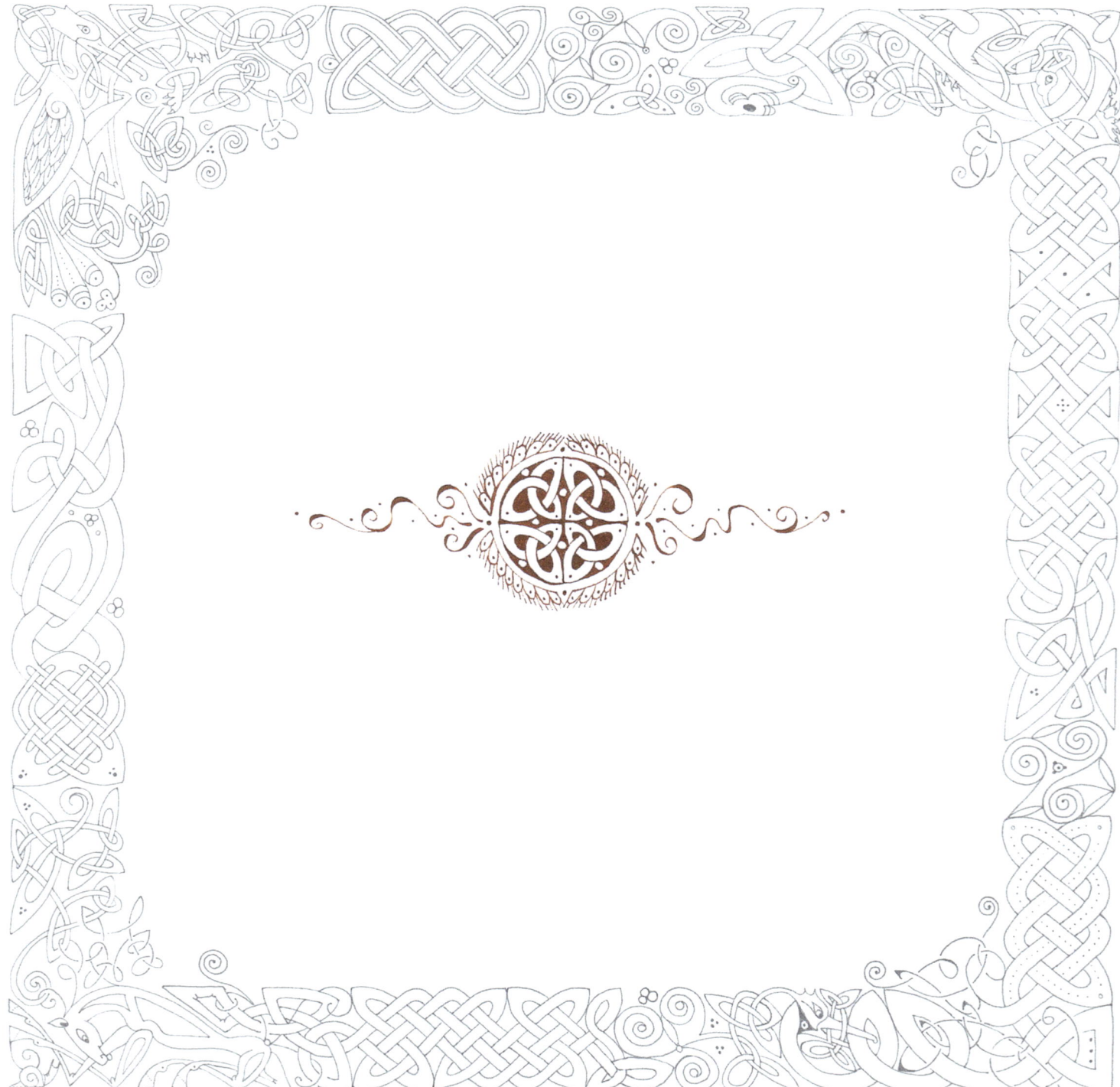

Carpet Page Projects

A Cross-Carpet-Page

When a page is entirely dedicated to intricate and interwoven design, it is known as a "Carpet Page". The Insular artists excelled at this art form, creating incredibly complex pages of knotwork, animals, spirals and other rich and detailed motifs.

For this somewhat simplified carpet-page, I chose a format of 17x15 cm, using a mottled paper in heathery mauve-grey.

Here you see the final design in its black & white stage, ready for colouring. Now, let's go through the steps to creating such a page, with interlace and zoömorphics...

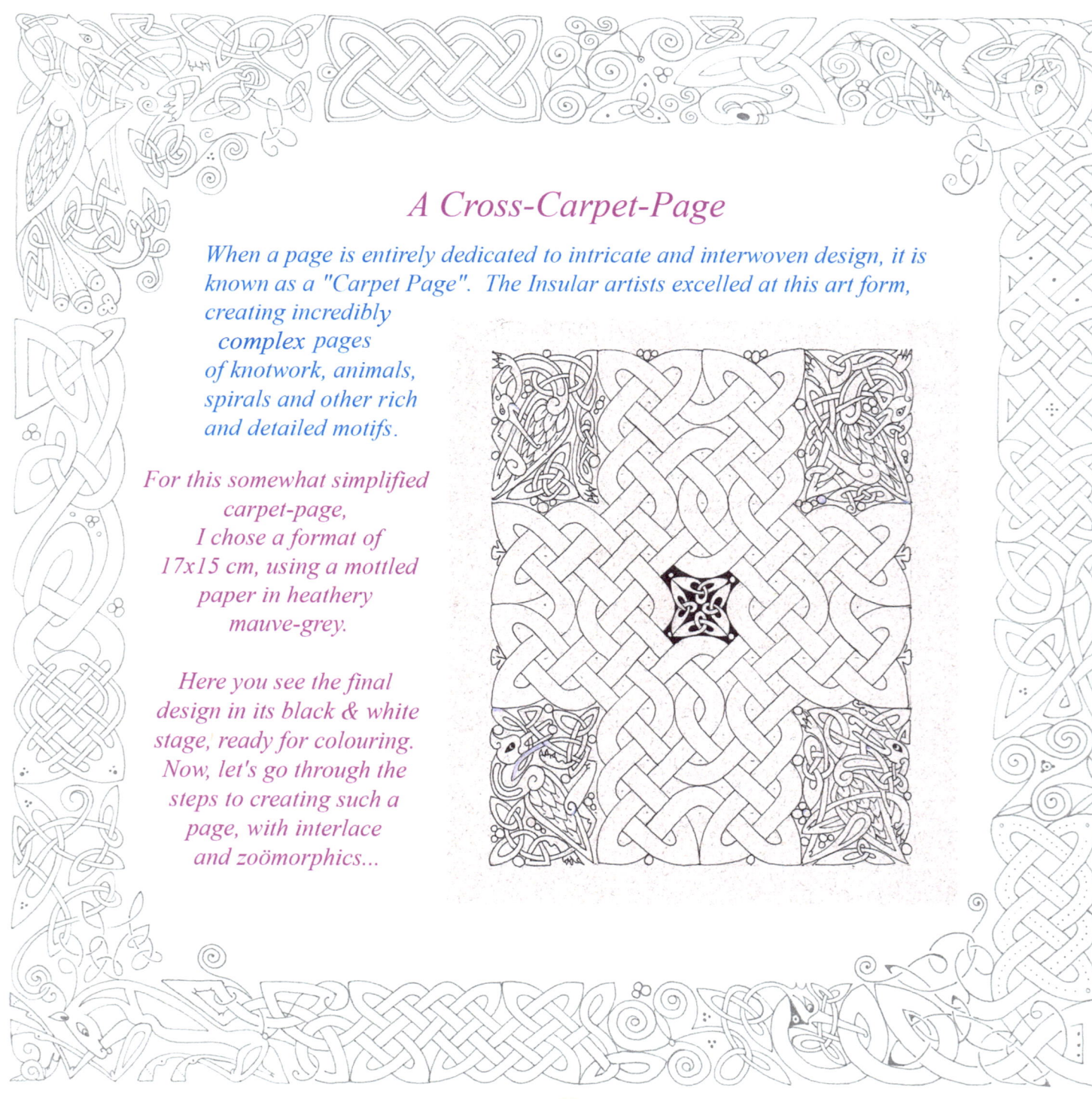

Step One: Page Lay-Out

The area for the cross is 15.5x12.5cm, thus leaving nice margins around the artwork. After pencilling-in this frame, I continued by indicating the centre of each side with a red dot.

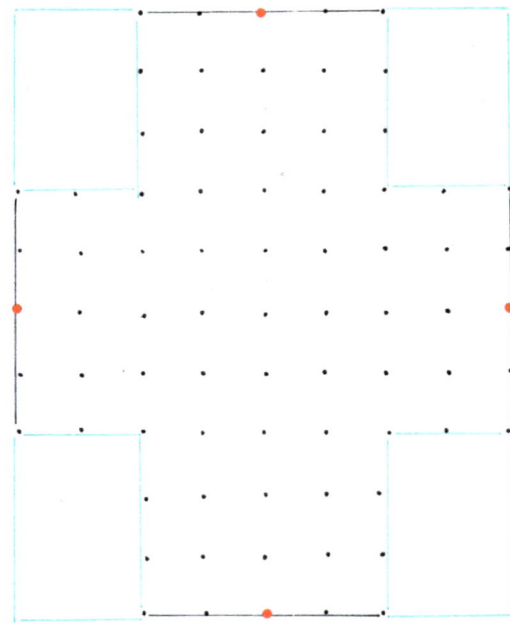

I then added dots at distances of 1.5cm: five dots at top and bottom, and five at each side. I made rows of dots, at the same distance, to fill-in the cross-shape. In pale blue marker I indicated the rectangles at each corner, to fill in later with birds.

Of course, you could work to another size or format. These dimensions are simply a suggestion for this practice-projet; but feel free to adapt them to your paper size and to your artistic preferences also!

This step was done in pen or marker, as all the dots and lines will be either covered in other colours or used as part of the final design.

Step Two: Inter-points and Pathways

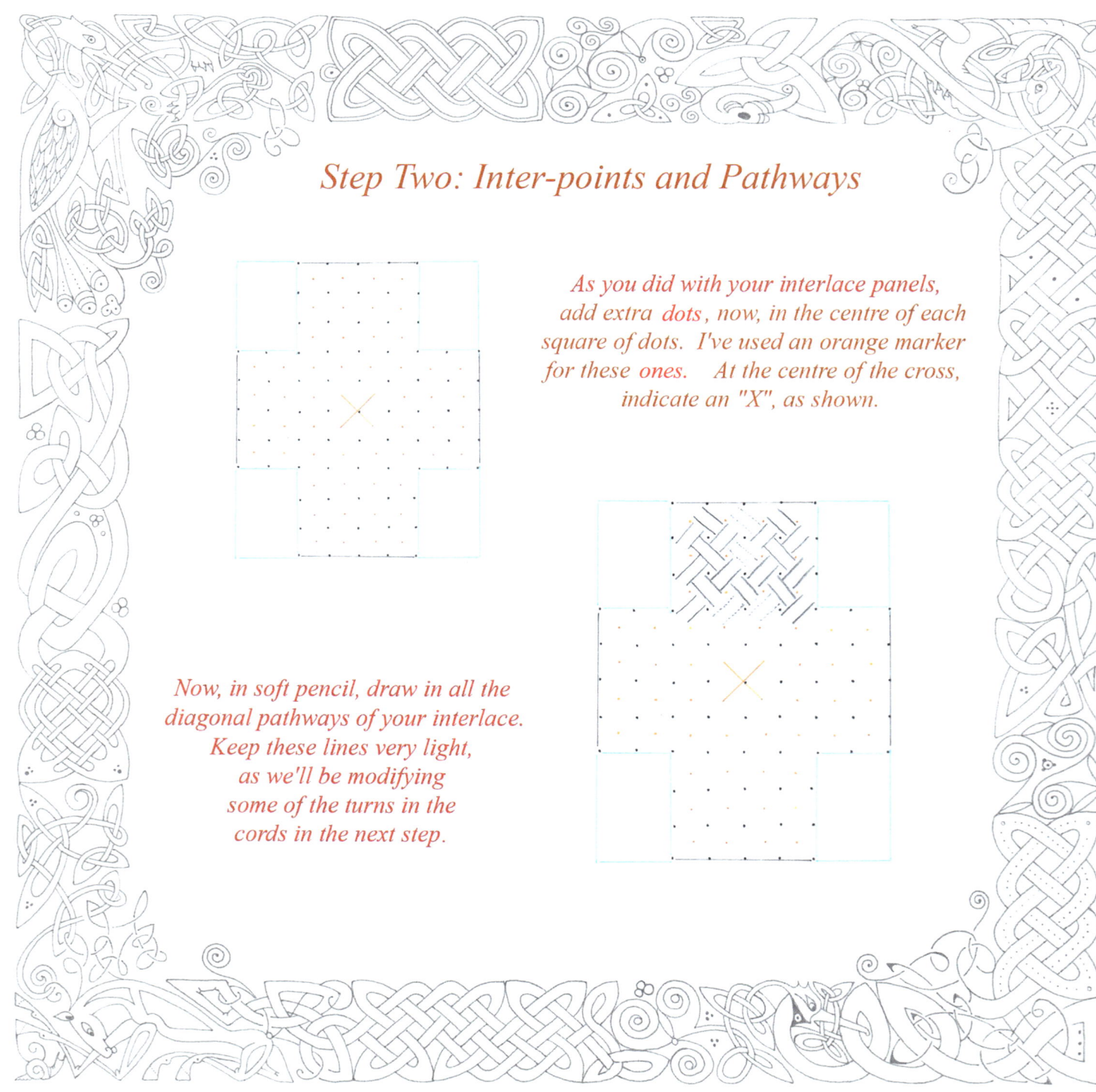

As you did with your interlace panels, add extra *dots*, now, in the centre of each square of dots. I've used an orange marker for these ones. At the centre of the cross, indicate an "X", as shown.

Now, in soft pencil, draw in all the diagonal pathways of your interlace. Keep these lines very light, as we'll be modifying some of the turns in the cords in the next step.

Step Three: Turns in the Path

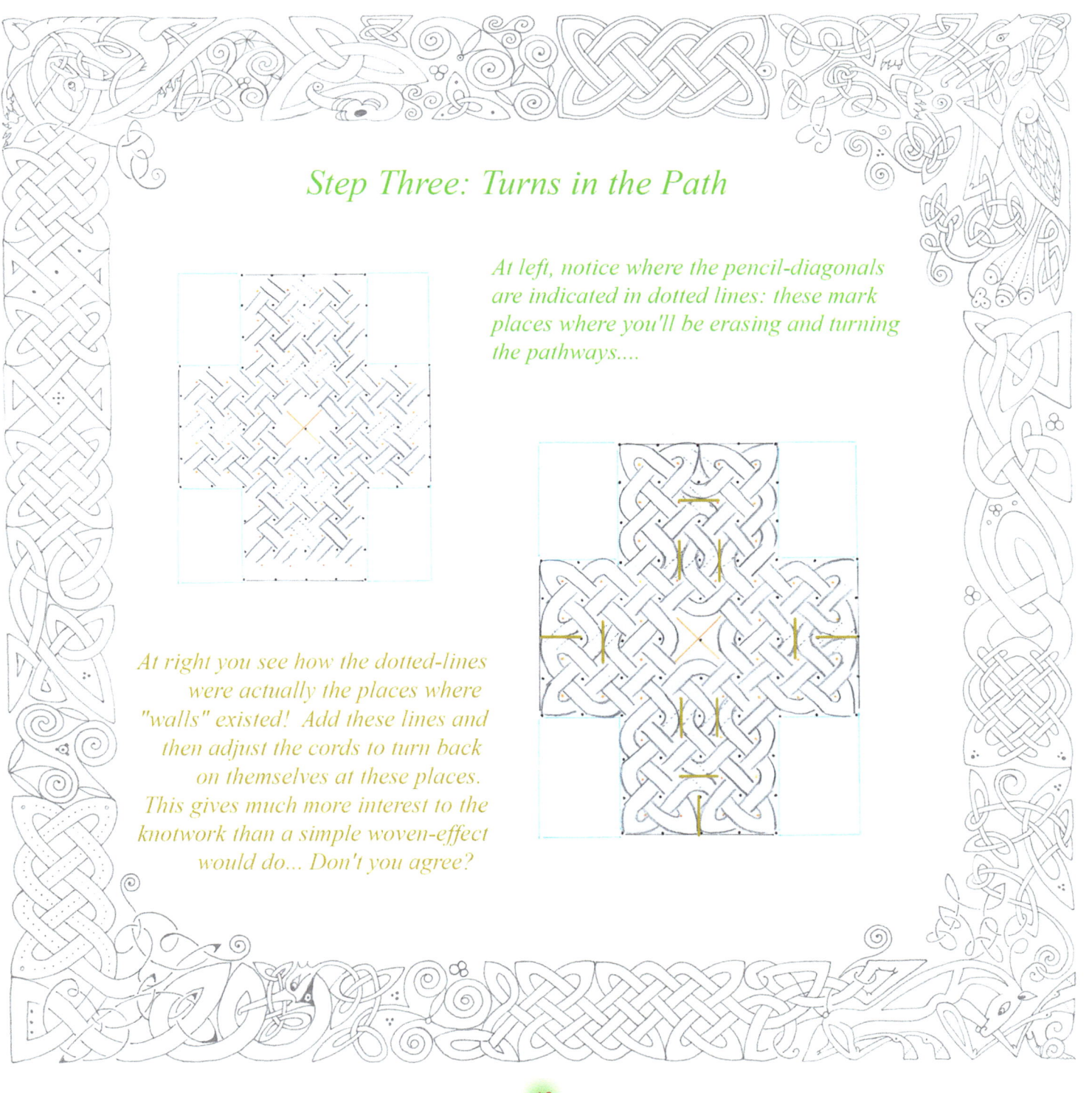

At left, notice where the pencil-diagonals are indicated in dotted lines: these mark places where you'll be erasing and turning the pathways....

At right you see how the dotted-lines were actually the places where "walls" existed! Add these lines and then adjust the cords to turn back on themselves at these places. This gives much more interest to the knotwork than a simple woven-effect would do... Don't you agree?

Step Four: Two of the Bird-Zoömorphics

You've already seen this bird, in Chapter 2, and now you're ready to draw him into the upper-left corner of your carpet page.

And below is the bird for the upper-right corner.
Please note that free-interlace cords (like all knotwork) must never have THREE pathways crossing at the same point, only two.
As you are drawing your knots around the bird's body, first in soft pencil of course, keep this rule in mind. By the way, the colours used in these examples are just to help you keep the forms clear --- they are really done in pencil, the intersections erased and then redrawn, and then they will be outlined in fine black felt-pen so that the pencil can be erased before colouring.

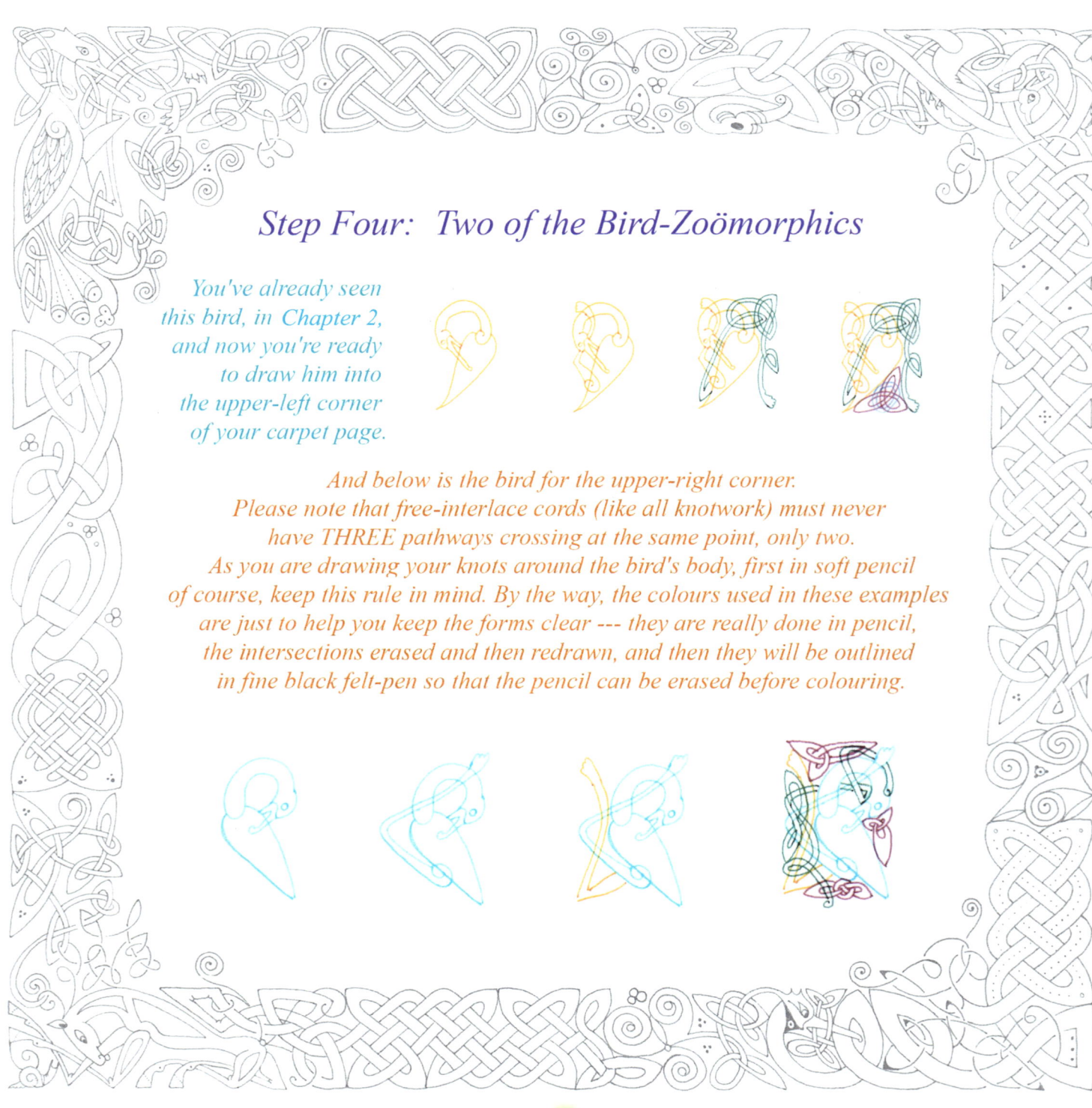

Step Five: Two More Birds

This is the bird at lower-left of our carpet page. The knot formed by his leg is indeed very complicated! Look for the main pathways, such as the long diagonal sweep of the leg or the semi-circle going through the beak. There is also a graceful half-circle in the lower leg (in blue). Good luck!

To finish, the bird in the lower-right is like a pelican, and at least his legs are less complicated than those of his brother-birds! However, other knots are required, indicated here in blue and orange. You may have practiced these birds on a separate sheet of paper --- if so, now is the time to put them into their four corners on your Cross Carpet-Page.

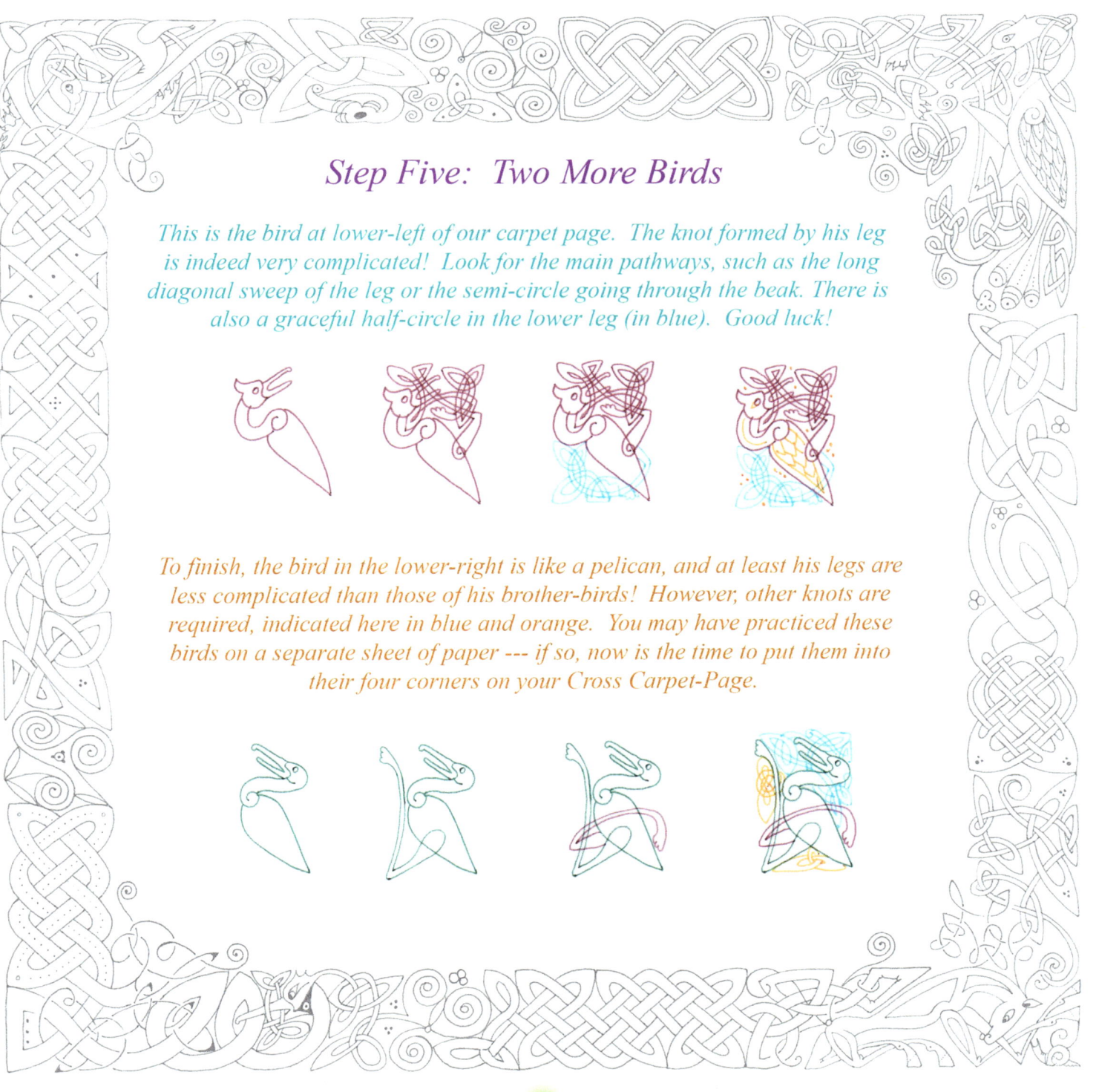

Step Six: The Central Motif

Here you have the steps to create the decoration at the centre of the cross.

1 --- This is the shape of the space left in the middle of the interlaced cords. Add four **dots** and connect them, in pencil, with curved lines following the contours as shown.

2 --- Draw these four little petals, which overlap the curved lines and touch in the middle of the central space.

3 --- From the points of the small petals, draw the larger petal-shapes which reach up to the four red dots.

5 --- Below you can see more clearly, in the final step, how the four motifs appear when the overs and unders have been neatly drawn. These triple-knots are very common in Celtic art: the Celts love the number three!

4 --- Now add the tiny triple loops which occupy the central petals and the two side ones of each part of the motif, formed here by purple and orange lines.

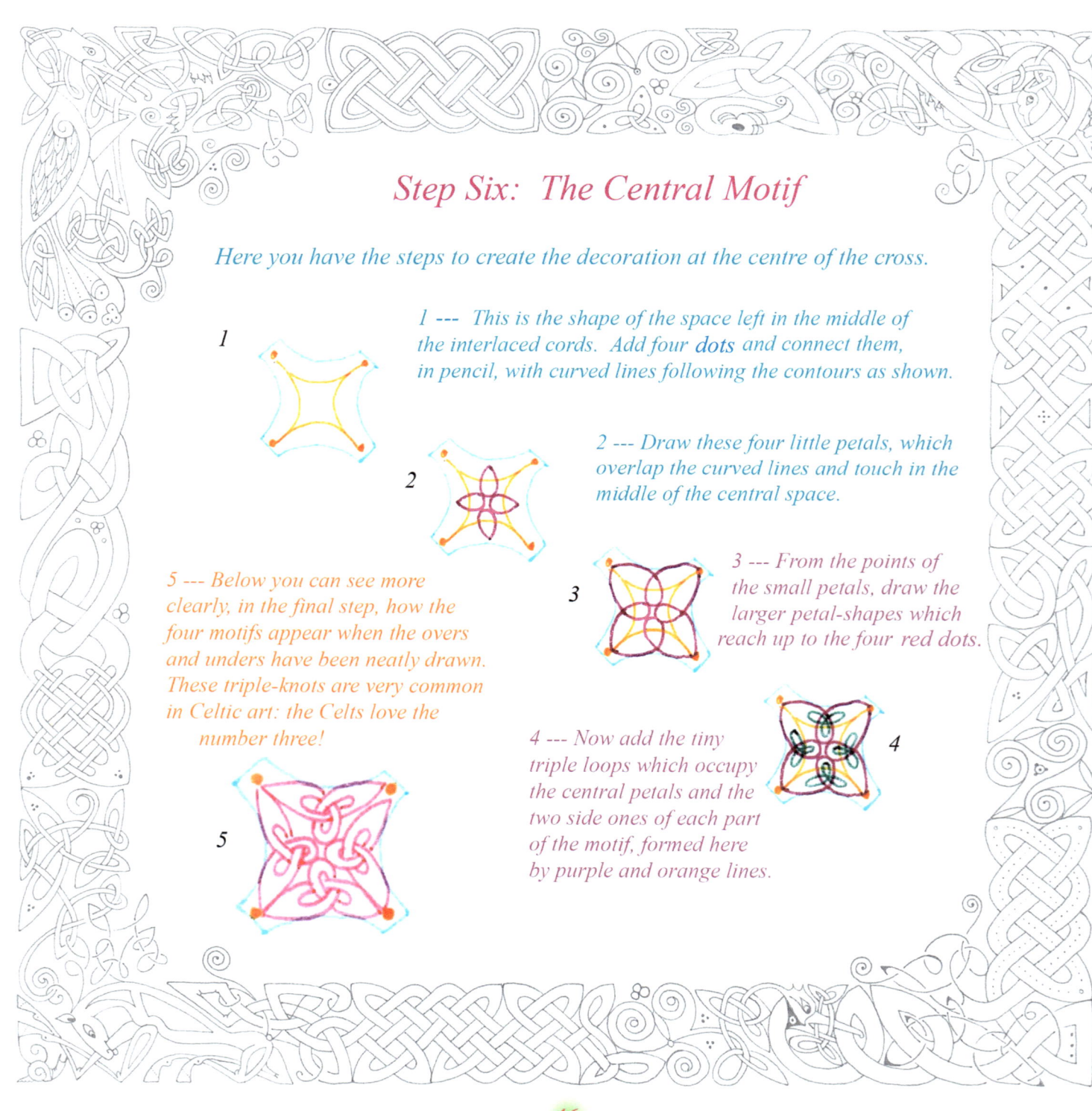

Step Seven: Colours Proposed

Before beginning to colour, I redrew all of the line-work in fine black felt-pen, erased the pencil, and filled-in the background of the cross in black.

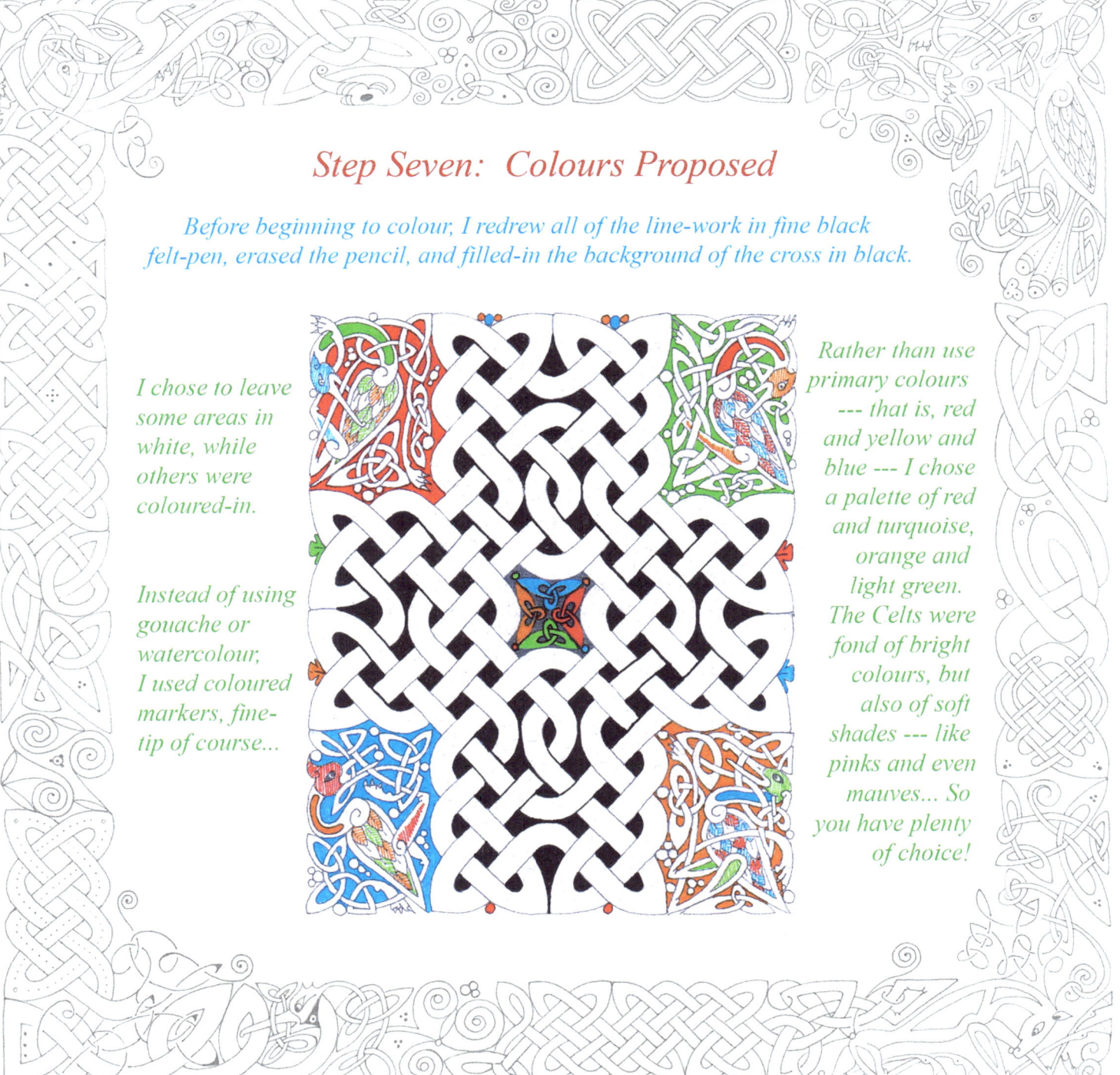

I chose to leave some areas in white, while others were coloured-in.

Instead of using gouache or watercolour, I used coloured markers, fine-tip of course...

Rather than use primary colours --- that is, red and yellow and blue --- I chose a palette of red and turquoise, orange and light green. The Celts were fond of bright colours, but also of soft shades --- like pinks and even mauves... So you have plenty of choice!

Sacred Symbolism

When new art styles and calligraphy arrived in Ireland, and other Celtic countries, from about the 5th century, they were at the service of a new religion: Christianity. The Celts already had a vast repertoire of motifs (spirals and animals, trumpet and step and key patterns, and knotwork of course).

Much of their creativity had been used in metalwork and stone-carving, but they soon mastered the writing and illuminating of manuscripts.

The Celtic Cross is rather unique, with its halo or sun-circle linking the four arms.

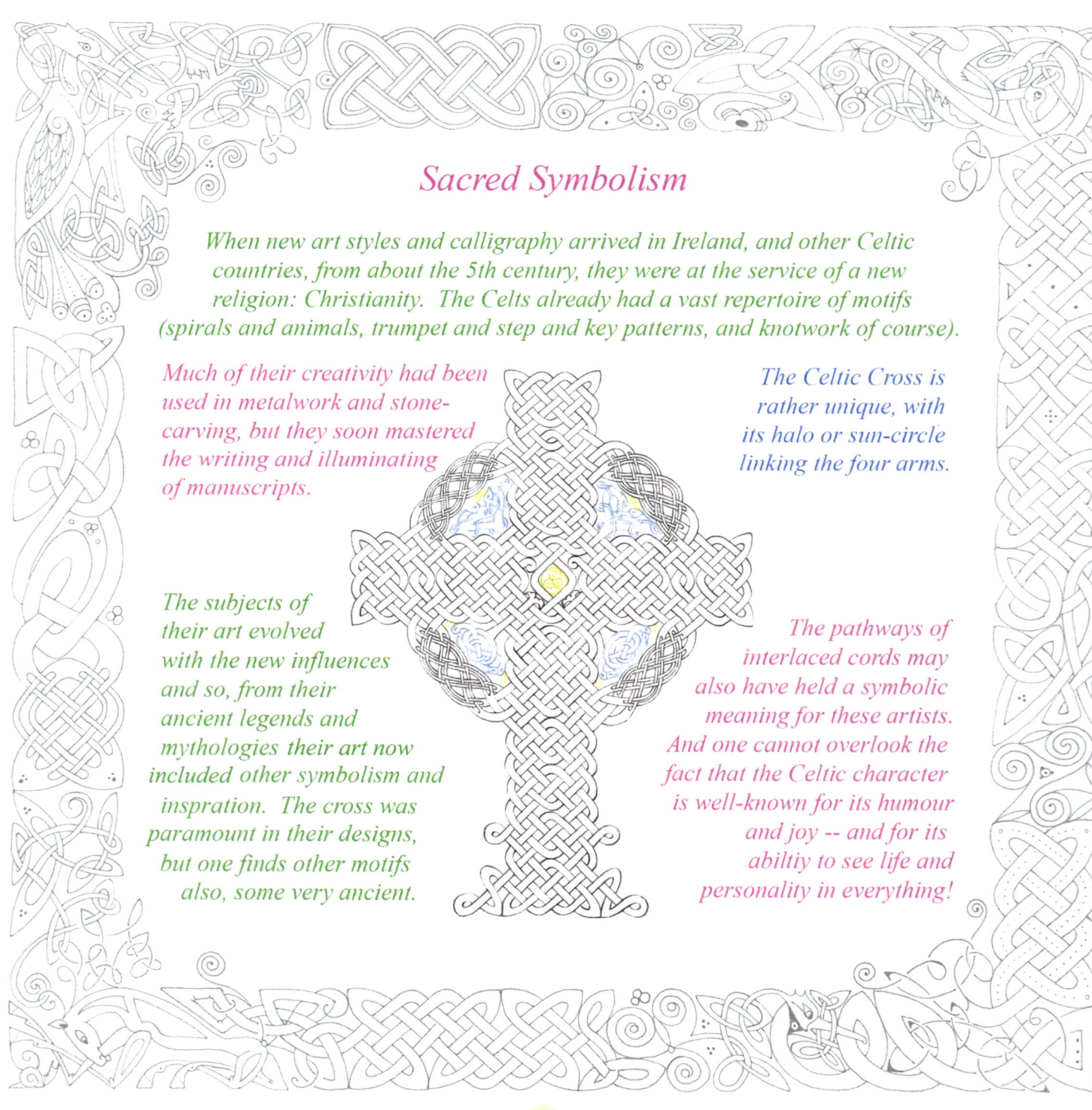

The subjects of their art evolved with the new influences and so, from their ancient legends and mythologies their art now included other symbolism and inspration. The cross was paramount in their designs, but one finds other motifs also, some very ancient.

The pathways of interlaced cords may also have held a symbolic meaning for these artists. And one cannot overlook the fact that the Celtic character is well-known for its humour and joy -- and for its abiltiy to see life and personality in everything!

The Celtic Cross

The form of the Celtic Cross is not only defined by its circular "halo", but also by its arms which radiate outwards. In this Carpet Page, I have outlined each section of the cross-form as if the whole design were actually cast in enamel, with separate 'compartments' for all the different parts..

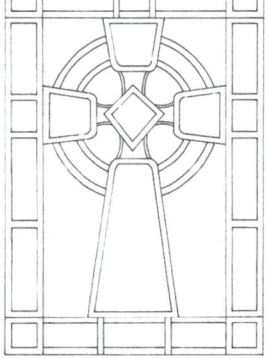

This is a very Insular practice: to separate each section of a design with firm outlines in black.

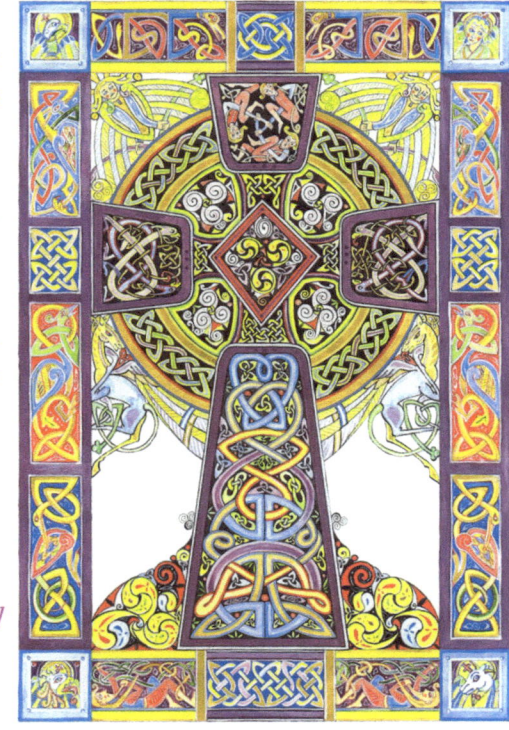

Rather un-historically, I've left two regions of white page showing through. Elsewhere, however, the motifs used to fill-in the compartments of this cross and its frame are very traditional: interlace, zoömorphics, spirals...

Painted in gouache, perfect for the art of illumination -- thanks to its opacity, most of the colours have been enhanced by the addition of very fine white lines or highlights, giving that extra sparkle to the piece!

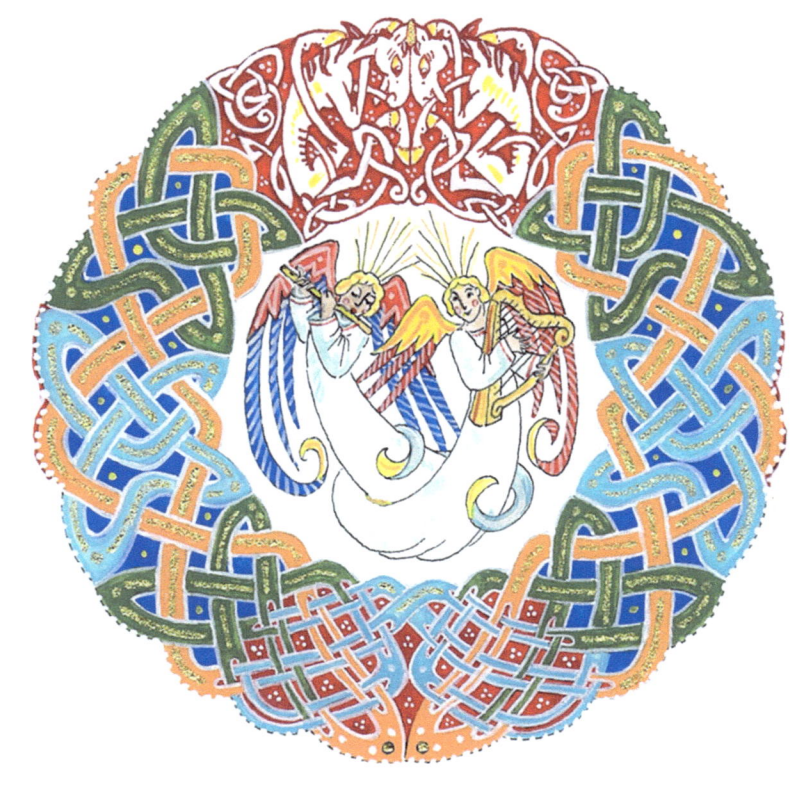

Other books by Jane Sullivan

Calligraphy - A Comprehensive Guide to Beautiful Lettering
Illuminated Letters Sketchbook
How to Draw Dragons
Unicorns - A Guide for Young Artists

Visit Jane's on-line Art School at   www.calligrafee.com/school